Amazing GRACE

GOD'S INITIATIVE—OUR RESPONSE

Timothy George

LifeWay Press
Nashville, Tennessee

ISBN 0-7673-9866-1

Dewey Decimal Classification Number: 234
Subject Heading: GRACE—THEOLOGY

This book is the text for course CG-0600 in the subject area Baptist Doctrine
in the Christian Growth Study Plan.

Unless otherwise noted, Scripture quotations are from the Holy Bible,
New International Version, copyright © 1973, 1978, 1984 by International Bible Society.

Scripture quotations marked NKJV are from the *New King James Version.*
Copyright ©1979, 1980, 1982, Thomas Nelson, Inc., Publishers.

Scripture quotations marked NASB are taken from the NEW AMERICAN STANDARD BIBLE,
© Copyright The Lockman Foundation, 1960, 1962, 1963, 1968, 1971, 1972, 1973, 1975, 1977, 1995.
Used by permission.

Scripture taken from **THE MESSAGE.** Copyright © by Eugene H. Peterson, 1993, 1994, 1995.
Used by permission of NavPress Publishing Group.

Scriptures reprinted with permission of Macmillan Publishing Co., from J. B. Phillips: *The New Testament in
Modern English,* Revised Edition. © J. B. Phillips 1958, 1960, 1972.

Scripture quotations marked NEB are from the *New English Bible,* © 1961, 1970 by the Delegates
of the Oxford University Press and the Syndics of the Cambridge University Press.

Scripture quotations marked KJV are from the *King James Version.*

To order additional copies of this resource: WRITE LifeWay Church Resources Customer Service, 127 Ninth
Avenue, North; Nashville, TN 37234-0113; FAX order to (615) 251-5933; PHONE 1-800-458; EMAIL to
customerservice@lifeway.com; or visit the LifeWay Christian Store serving you.

Don Atkinson, Editor • Robert Redden, Art Director • Pam Shepherd, Assistant Editor
• Leslie Irwin, Manuscript Assistant

LifeWay.
Printed in the United States of America
127 Ninth Avenue, North
Nashville, Tennessee 37234-0151

*As God works through us, we will help people and churches know Jesus Christ and seek His kingdom
by providing biblical solutions that spiritually transform individuals and cultures.*

CONTENTS

ABOUT THE AUTHOR

Dr. Timothy George is the founding dean of Beeson Divinity School of Samford University. Prior to coming to Samford, he served as professor of Church History and Historical Theology at The Southern Baptist Theological Seminary. A native of Chattanooga, he holds degrees from the University of Tennessee at Chattanooga (B.A.), Harvard Divinity School (M.Div.), and Harvard University (Th.D.).

A noted historian and theologian, Dr. George has written and edited numerous books including *Theology of the Reformers, Baptist Theologians, Faithful Witness: The Life and Mission of William Carey,* and the *New American Commentary on Galatians.* Dr. George serves as senior editor for *Christianity Today* and is a member of the editorial boards of Books and Culture and Harvard Theological Review. George also chairs the Theological Education Committee of the Baptist World Alliance and is a widely sought-after speaker on matters of Christian higher education, theological and biblical issues, and cultural trends.

He is married to Denise George, a prolific author in her own right; they have two children—Christian and Alyce. The Georges are members of Shades Mountain Baptist Church in Birmingham, Alabama.

PREFACE

"For it is by grace you have been saved,
through faith—and this not from yourselves,
it is the gift of God—not by works,
so that no one can boast" (Eph. 2:8-9).

Amazing Grace is the 2001 Doctrine Study for the Southern Baptist Convention. This year's study focuses on one of the most basic themes of the Christian faith—the amazing grace of God. Grace is the great theme of the Bible from first to last. *Sola gratia,* "by grace alone," is the most fundamental affirmation of the Reformation and of all true evangelical Christianity. John Bunyan's great master-piece of the spiritual life, *The Pilgrim's Progress,* tells the story of a man who set out from home carrying a great burden. Someone named Evangelist pointed him toward a celestial city shining in the distance. Along the way, the man lost his burden and, though there were many struggles and battles yet to come, he was sustained through them all by the unlimited love of God. The burden in the story is sin. The city of light is heaven. Before he left home, the man's name was Graceless. When his burden was lifted, his name became Christian. Christian's story is our story too. We are saved by grace alone, through faith alone, in Jesus Christ alone. And in that same grace we walk, step by step, toward that "city with foundations, whose architect and builder is God" (Heb. 11:10).

As wonderful as grace is, it has provoked some of the most heated controversies in the history of the Christian church. In this study, we shall look at some of these debated questions while never losing sight, I trust, of the reality we're discussing: God's free and sovereign favor to ill-deserving sinners. God's great ocean of truth is so much deeper than our finite minds can fathom. I am keenly aware that there is much more to be said about grace than I have been able to say in this brief study. My purpose throughout has been more devotional than academic: God's grace should provoke wonder and worship among all God's children.

I want to thank those whose kindness and encouragement have helped me to write this book. Don Atkinson, who served as editor of this project, invited me to write on this theme and has provided courteous and able support at every step. Amy Corbin, my administrative secretary, worked efficiently in preparing the manuscript for press. My colleagues at Beeson Divinity School and Samford University have been wonderful discussion partners and co-laborers in the Lord's work. My wife, Denise, and our children, Christian and Alyce, have taught me a lot about grace and forgiveness, and I love them very much. This book is dedicated to two of my former students who serve as Southern Baptist missionaries in Thailand.

This is my prayer: May this study be used to draw us all closer to the heart of God, and may our lives overflow with gratitude, until, in the words of Charles Wesley's great hymn, we find ourselves "lost in wonder, love, and praise."

Soli Deo Gloria!
Timothy George
Epiphany, 2000

For

Mark and Jackie DeVine

Trophies of grace
and heralds of Christ
in the worthy tradition
of Anne and Adoniram

CHAPTER ONE

Our Gracious God

Great God of wonders!
All thy ways Are worthy of
thyself—divine:
And the bright glories of thy
grace Among thine other
wonders shine;
Who is a pardoning God like
thee? Or who has grace
so rich and free?
—Samuel Davies

If you were asked to sum up the Bible's entire message in just one word, which word would you choose? Reconciliation, salvation, justification, atonement, faith, love, eternity? All of these are wonderful words, but the word I would choose is *grace.* The very last verse in the Bible summarizes the message of Holy Scripture from Genesis to Revelation: "The grace of our Lord Jesus Christ be with you all" (Rev. 22:21, NKJV).

The word *grace* is found some 150 times in the New Testament alone. A quick look in any Bible concordance will show how "grace" is used to describe the most basic truths of the Christian faith. The God of the Bible is preeminently the God of grace (see 1 Pet. 5:10). Jesus came into the world "full of grace and truth" (John 1:14). The Holy Spirit is the "spirit of grace" (Zech. 12:10). God's throne is "the throne of grace" (Heb. 4:16). We receive forgiveness "in accordance with the riches of God's grace" (Eph. 1:7). We are chosen, justified, sanctified and one day we will be glorified all because of grace. Every Christian is called to be a good steward of the manifold grace of God (see 1 Pet. 4:10). God's grace "brings salvation" (Titus 2:11). The good news we proclaim is the gospel of grace and if anyone preaches a different gospel, Paul does not hesitate to say, in the boldest language imaginable, that person should be eternally condemned (see Gal. 1:6-9).

PERSONAL LEARNING ACTIVITY
Write your own definition of grace or one you have heard that is especially meaningful to you.

_____

_____

Grace is the great theme of the Bible, and it is also present in every act of Christian worship and devotion. We say "grace" at the table before we eat our meals. Christian baptism celebrates the triumph of God's grace in bringing a lost man or woman out of the darkness of sin into the marvelous light of new life in Christ. In the Lord's Supper we remember God's gracious favor in sending Christ to be our Redeemer, even as we commune with Him through the power of the Holy Spirit and look forward to the marriage supper of the Lamb when, by God's grace, we shall see the Savior face-to-face. Frequently our worship services are closed by a benediction extolling the triune God of grace and love: "May the grace of the Lord Jesus Christ, and the love of God, and the fellowship of the Holy Spirit be with you all" (2 Cor. 13:14).

Christians love to sing about God's grace! *Marvelous, infinite, matchless grace, Freely bestowed on all who believe.*[1] When I was a teenager I often listened to a radio broadcast called Revival Time with evangelist C.M. Ward. In every program, as Dr. Ward gave the gospel invitation, the choir sang: "The cross upon which Jesus died Is a shelter in which we can hide; And its grace so free is sufficient for me, And deep is its fountain, as wide as the sea. There's room at the cross for you. …"[2]

But no hymn is more beloved than John Newton's "Amazing Grace! How Sweet the Sound." The son of a British shipmaster, Newton entered into naval service himself and became a slave trader. Amidst the perils of the sea, he was rescued from a life of despair and debauchery. Newton later became, along with William Wilberforce, a major force in the abolition of the slave trade. In looking back on his life, and the transformation that had occurred, he could account for this change only by appealing to the grace of God. He wrote:

> Amazing Grace! how sweet the sound,
> That saved a wretch like me!
> I once was lost, but now am found,
> Was blind, but now I see.

On any given Sunday you can still hear it sung in great cathedrals and in small country churches, on the radio and television, by gospel quartets and operatic soloists, in hundreds of languages around the world:

> 'Twas grace that taught my heart to fear,
> And grace my fears relieved;
> How precious did that grace appear
> The hour I first believed!

The doctrine of grace raises many questions.

There is a sense in which God's grace is so simple that even a small child can grasp its meaning. And yet it is so profound that the most learned theologians cannot fully comprehend its wonder and beauty and power. For grace is not only amazing, it is also perplexing. When we think about it, and God does want us to think about it (see 2 Tim. 2:15), the doctrine of grace raises many questions in our minds. From what source comes God's grace? If it is true that humans can do nothing to save themselves, why are there so many commands and exhortations in the Bible? What about predestination? How does God's sovereignty relate to human responsibility? Is the invitation to believe in Christ really meant for everyone—or just the chosen elect? What about falling from grace? Is it possible to lose our salvation by falling into sin? Does God really know everything that happens before it occurs? If God is sovereign, why do suffering and evil exist in the world? How should we understand the grace of God in relation to missions and evangelism? Why is election or predestination sometimes a source of division, even among Bible-believing Christians?

We will deal with these questions as well as some others in this study. But I want to make clear right from the start that I do not claim to offer completely satisfactory answers to all these questions. The apostle Paul had personal revelations and visitations to heaven not available to other Christians. But even he was forced to admit that "we know in part and we prophesy in part ... Now we see but a poor reflection as in a mirror" (1 Cor. 13:9,12). The study of God's grace is like staring into the sun on a bright cloudless day: it's a dangerous thing to do. Our eyes can be damaged, even blinded by such unobstructed vision. Yet only by means of the sun can we see anything at all—the blue sky, beautiful flowers, mountains, meadows, all of God's multicolored creation. Only a stupid person would decide to live his entire life inside a bunker beneath the ground for fear of walking outside in the sunshine. And so with God's grace, we must not peer too directly into matters God has not revealed so clearly, lest our spiritual vision be blurred. But we must never forget that only by God's grace can we see anything at all. May God—a God who is far greater than our best ideas, and infinitely more marvelous than our finest theologies—help us to approach this subject with reverence, humility, and a sense of wonder.

We should approach the subject of God's grace with reverence, humility, and a sense of wonder.

I recognize that not everyone will agree with the answers I shall offer on some of these disputed matters. Thus in the interest of full disclosure, let me say up-front that I write from the perspective of a Reformed Baptist theologian. This view, I believe, represents the mainstream of historic Baptist theology through the centuries. My views on God's grace do not differ from those held by such evangelically committed and missionary-minded Baptist leaders as John Bunyan, Roger Williams, William Carey, Andrew Fuller, Luther Rice, Adoniram Judson, and Charles Haddon Spurgeon.

In fairness, though, it needs to be said that there has always been within the Baptist tradition a variety of views on how God's grace should be understood, on the proper balance between divine sovereignty and human responsibility. Throughout this study, I shall note areas of significant divergence while disclosing my own views as well. Evangelical Christians committed to historic Christian orthodoxy, whether Calvinists or Arminians, share more in common about the doctrine of grace than their disputes and battles have some-times shown. I want to emphasize this common ground, for it may be blurred by zealous combatants on both sides. At the same time, I want to encourage all of us to a deeper searching of God's Word on this crucial doctrine. Tertullian indicated that the Christians of ancient Carthage maintained a certain reputation among the pagans of that city: "See, they say, how they love one another."[3] When the world looks at the church today, what it needs most is not to see Christians conducting graceless debates about the doctrine of grace. What the world needs to see is believers transformed by grace, loving one another, and reaching out to a lost world in Jesus' name.

In recent years, there has been a lively discussion of these issues among many Baptists, and I think this is a good thing. In some measure, this discussion has been prompted by the return to a sounder doctrine of biblical authority. If the Bible really is the Word of God, inerrant and infallible in all that it claims, then it becomes very important to determine exactly what the Bible does teach about such important matters as God's grace and our response to it. While Baptists may not agree on every aspect of interpretation, at the end of the day we will submit our judgment to the final bar of Holy Scripture. We are grateful for Baptist heroes of the past, and we may rightly turn to them for guidance. But Conner, Hobbs, Mullins, Strong, Spurgeon, Broadus, Boyce, and the other theologians whose works we can read with much profit, may sometimes be wrong on this or that matter of doctrine. From first to last, our warrant is God's Word! Like the disciples of Berea, we must examine the Scriptures to see whether these things are true (see Acts 17:11).

Like Martin Luther at the Diet of Worms, may our consciences remain captive to the Holy Scriptures.

What Grace Is

There are many definitions of grace, but one of my favorites is the one I first learned as a little boy in Sunday School: Grace is *God's Riches at Christ's Expense*. We must not stumble over the simplicity of the phrase lest we also miss its profundity. It points to three elements which are essential in a biblical understanding of grace. First, grace originates with God. God initiates grace. As Paul said in Romans 9:16: "It does not, therefore, depend on man's desire or effort, but on God's mercy." If any creature has any claim on grace whatsoever, it is solely because that grace has been given, bestowed, freely and undeservedly granted by God. Second, God's grace is inexhaustible, irrepressible, overflowing. God is not stingy. He is "rich in mercy," Paul said (Eph. 2:4). Once a violent persecutor of God's people, a converted Paul declared that "the grace of our Lord was poured out on me abundantly" (1 Tim. 1:14). When John Bunyan wrote his own spiritual autobiography, he picked up on this same theme calling his book *Grace Abounding to the Chief of Sinners* (see Rom. 5:20). One of the problems with the term "limited atonement" is that it suggests that something is missing or lacking in God's grace. Like cold drinks at a picnic, the supply has to be "limited" for fear that it might run out, that there might not be enough to go around! But this could not possibly be true for God's grace, for it is infinite and knows no such bounds. Finally, grace is God's riches—*at Christ's expense*. We should never think of grace apart from Jesus Christ. Jesus is the incarnate Son of God, the enfleshment of divine grace. This means that while grace is radically free, it is never cheap for it cost God the dearest thing He had—the sacrifice of His Son.

In chapter 3 we will study the theme of God's sovereignty in salvation, but it is equally important to stress the sovereign freedom of God in creation as well. We cannot understand grace without considering this question: Who is God and why did He make the world in the first place? Some people teach that God made the world because, way back in the vast reaches of eternity past, He had somehow grown lonely. He created the world, so this theory goes, in order to have something to love. What an utterly pagan notion of God! It supposes that in His innermost being, God lives utterly alone—a monad, superior and transcendent to be sure, but isolated and aloof in His omnipotence. Arius, a false teacher of the fourth century, believed this. He wrote, "We know there is one God, alone unbegotten, alone eternal, alone without beginning, alone true, alone immortal."[4]

The Bible provides a very different picture of God. Here we learn that within the being of God Himself lies a mysterious living love, a dynamic reciprocity of surrender and

It is "from the fullness of his grace we have all received one blessing after another" (John 1:16).

13

affirmation, of giving and receiving, among the Father, the Son, and the Holy Spirit. God is not the Alone with the Alone. The Maker of heaven and earth is both unipersonal and tripersonal. He is the triune God of holiness and love.

God does not express His ultimate reality in terms of brute power and force alone. This is not the most decisive mark of God's divinity. The relationship of total and mutual self-giving, by which the Father gives everything to the Son, and the Son offers back all that He has to glorify the Father, is what makes God really God. The love of the Father and the Son for each other is established and sealed by the Holy Spirit who proceeds from both.

God did not make the world because He had to, but simply because He chose to do so.

If all this is true, then why on earth did God make the world in the first place? Not because He had to, but simply because He chose to, for His "good pleasure," as Paul put it (Eph. 1:5, NKJV). Contrary to the thinking of certain feminist theologians, God is the Lord of creation, not its midwife. God did not need to create something outside of Himself as an object for His love, for "God is love" (1 John 4:8). There is nothing missing or lacking in God. He is the fountain of being. In Him dwells all holiness, glory, light, power, happiness, joy. Yet amazingly, out of the richness and utter sufficiency of His own being, God created the world and human beings within it. He granted them a creaturely reality and freedom and invited them to share in the outpouring of His divine love for all eternity. Indeed, the Bible speaks of God as "jealous" for His own glory and honor. He will brook no rivals. But He is not a grudging, stingy God like a Silas Marner carefully counting his gold coins every night for fear that one of them might have gotten away. No, at the heart of God springs freedom, a generosity which reflects His own character. This forms the basis of all human reality and freedom. This kindles the source of wonder and awe, the kind of wonder which prompted Martin Luther to find sermons in peach stones and to adore the living God who made heaven and earth (and me too, Luther said), "of sheer fatherly kindness and compassion, apart from any merit or worthiness

14

of mine; for all of which I am bound to thank and praise Him, to serve Him and to be obedient, which is assuredly true."[5]

Some people accept the idea that God created the world, but they cannot imagine that He has much to do with its continuing operation, much less with our human lives. The British poet and novelist, Thomas Hardy, once wrote in disparaging terms about God as "the dreaming, dark, dumb Thing that turns the handle of this idle Show."[6] Hardy believed in the god of deism: He created the world, and still cranks it along from time to time, but he wouldn't think of getting his hands dirty in the daily muck and mess of it all. He is like an absentee landlord who neither knows nor cares much about the tenants who occupy his property. An idol of the modern imagination, this god has crippled feet and withered hands, eyes that don't see, and ears that don't hear.

How different is the God of the Bible who is everywhere— active, alive, involved. Jesus said that no act was too minute or insignificant for the Father's care. He knows every time a sparrow falls to the ground in a hailstorm. In His great and boundless wisdom, God even knows how to do good using evil instruments, including the devil himself. Paul made this clear in 2 Corinthians 12:7, where he described the "thorn in my flesh" as something "given" by God through "a messenger of Satan." Through God's providential care, even painful episodes such as this can become occasions for grace.

Common Grace

When we think of God's general providence and care for the world and all its creatures, we are talking about *common grace* as distinguished from the *special grace* of God manifested in the coming of Christ into the world to save sinners. We can see evidence of God's common grace in His general revelation—God's disclosure of His reality throughout the created world and also in the human conscience. In speaking to a pagan audience at Lystra, Paul declared that God "has not left himself without testimony: He has shown kindness by giving you rain from heaven and crops in their seasons; he provides

Common grace is God's general providence and care for the world.

15

you with plenty of food and fills your hearts with joy" (Acts 14:17). God pours His common grace out indiscriminately on all persons everywhere, causing the sun to shine and the rain to fall on the just and the unjust alike (see Matt. 5:45).

God's common grace also serves as a restraining force against the demonic powers of evil which, if left to their own devices, would wreak such havoc on earth that human life would be impossible. All political order, social stability, and family cohesiveness would be overturned in a moment without the nurture of God's sustaining grace. In this sense, Paul referred to government as an authority "instituted" by God. A civil ruler is "God's servant," that is, His agent for equity and justice in the world (Rom. 13:2-4), even though such a person may have no personal knowledge of God as Redeemer. All that is good and tolerable in human life, all that is noble and praiseworthy in the realms of politics, culture, science, art, music, literature—for all of this we may thank God. And also for His common grace, reflected in His "longsuffering" and patience toward His wayward creation (see 2 Pet. 3:9, NKJV).

Some teach that common grace and general revelation alone are sufficient to bring lost persons into a saving relationship with God. However, nothing in the Bible supports this theory. On the contrary, the Scriptures teach that human beings everywhere have abused and corrupted the natural knowledge of God implanted in their souls. Again and again, they have turned from the knowledge of God revealed in nature and in conscience and have worshiped and served false gods, idols, even demons rather than submitting to the one true and living God of creation (see Rom. 1:18-31). This was as true in the Old Testament as in the New, as the prophet Isaiah made clear: "Though grace is shown to the wicked, they do not learn righteousness; even in a land of uprightness they go on doing evil and regard not the majesty of the Lord" (Isa. 26:10).

The verdict of Scripture is clear: God's presence and power are evidenced in every human heart through the witness of common grace. This testimony renders every single person inexcusable before the bar of God's righteous judgment. But

> **God's revelation of Himself in the created order is not all that is required for salvation.**

true salvation and eternal life, that is, deliverance from sin and death, comes about only through the interposition of God's special, redemptive grace.

Salvation comes only through God's special, redemptive grace.

PERSONAL LEARNING ACTIVITY

How are common grace and special grace alike?

_____

How are common grace and special grace different?

_____

God's Long-Range Plan

Oscar Hardman once wrote that the doctrine of grace "is profound in its nature, wide in its scope, comprehensive in its bearings, forbidding in its possession of a technical terminology, and confusing in the variety of the formulations which its successive exponents have given to it."[7] Surely he is right! Even Paul, the great apostle of grace, often stretched the capacity of human language to its breaking point in describing the boundless love and grace of God. Right in the middle of his letter to the Ephesians, he interrupted his discussion of salvation by grace to conduct a prayer meeting. He actually fell on his knees and prayed to the Father. He asked that the Christians to whom he was writing would be able to grasp the extravagant dimensions of his subject. Who can experience its breadth, he asked? Or measure its length, or plumb its depths, or soar up to its heights? He wanted them to understand the full extent of God's grace, not just intellectually, but experientially. He wanted them "to know it, though it is beyond knowledge" (Eph. 3:18, NEB).

One of the grandest statements of the overarching structure of divine grace comes at the very beginning of Ephesians. Here Paul described its comprehensive content as well as its encompassing reach. Ephesians 1:3-14 is just one

In Christ we are given forgiveness of sin, and a new identity in His redemptive plan.

sentence in the Greek New Testament, perhaps the longest sentence in the Bible! So rich and complex is Paul's thought that one struggles to translate this as a single sentence in English. The *King James Version*, using colons, divides it into three complete sentences; the *New International Version*, eight. Eugene H. Peterson renders it this way in his popular translation, *The Message*:

How blessed is God! And what a blessing he is! He's the Father of our Master, Jesus Christ, and takes us to the high places of blessing in him. Long before he laid down earth's foundations, he had us in mind, had settled on us as the focus of his love, to be made whole and holy by his love. Long, long ago he decided to adopt us into his family through Jesus Christ. (What pleasure he took in planning this!) He wanted us to enter into the celebration of his lavish gift-giving by the hand of his beloved Son.

Because of the sacrifice of the Messiah, his blood poured out on the altar of the Cross, we're a free people—free of penalties and punishments chalked up by all our misdeeds. And not just barely free, either. Abundantly free! He thought of everything, provided for everything we could possibly need, letting us in on the plans he took such delight in making. He set it all out before us in Christ, a long-range plan in which everything would be brought together and summed up in him, everything in deepest heaven, everything on planet earth.

It's in Christ that we find out who we are and what we are living for. Long before we first heard of Christ and got our hopes up, he had his eye on us, had designs on us for glorious living, part of the overall purpose he is working out in everything and everyone.

It's in Christ that you, once you heard the truth and believed it (this Message of your salvation), found yourselves home free— signed, sealed, and delivered by the Holy Spirit. This signet from God is the first installment on what's coming, a reminder that we'll get everything God has planned for us, a praising and glorious life (Eph. 1:3-14).

This passage begins and ends with praise to God. In between the praise for God, Paul places our Christian calling and everything related to it in the context of God's eternal purpose—His long-range plan stretching from the very first nana-second of creation through the final cry of victory at the end of time. He does this by identifying four "moments" in God's plan of salvation. We can depict Paul's theology of grace as a continuum with four distinct but interrelated moments which derive both their unity and their uniqueness from God's free and sovereign grace. If, for the sake of clarity, we call these moments *metahistorical, historical, experiential,* and *eschatological,* then the continuum may be illustrated as follows:

His long-range plan stretches from the very first nana-second of creation through the final cry of victory at the end of time.

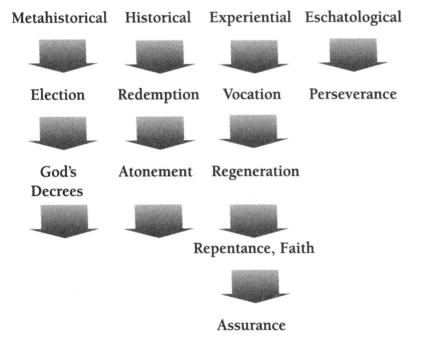

Metahistorical	Historical	Experiential	Eschatological
Election	Redemption	Vocation	Perseverance
God's Decrees	Atonement	Regeneration	
	Repentance, Faith		
	Assurance		

Let's look briefly at each of these four ways of situating grace within the overall plan of salvation.

1. *Metahistorical.* This word means "above history" or "prior to history." Paul said that God established His purpose of grace even before the creation of the world: "Long before he

Jesus enjoyed an intimate relationship with the Father before the beginning of time.

laid down earth's foundations, he had us in mind, had settled on us as the focus of his love, to be made whole and holy by his love" (Eph. 1:4-5, *The Message*). Admittedly, eternity remains a difficult topic for a finite mind to grasp, and we must be careful not to speculate beyond what God has revealed to us in His Word. An eager student once asked St. Augustine what he thought God was doing before He made the world. To this question the great theologian replied, with a twinkle in his eye perhaps, that God was busy creating hell for overly curious souls! Certainly there is much about the eternal decrees (the technical term for God's pre-temporal decision) about which we do not know and may never learn.

But from time to time throughout the Bible, God Himself pulls back the curtain of eternity and gives us a glimpse into the inner sanctum of His divine life in eternity past. For example, Jesus spoke of the intimate relationship He enjoyed with the Father "before the world began" (John 17:5) and "before the creation of the world" (John 17:24). Jesus also declared that God had been preparing a kingdom for His elect children "from the foundation of the world" (Matt. 25:34, NKJV). Peter tells us that Christ was foreordained "before the creation of the world" to be a spotless sacrifice for sin (1 Pet. 1:18-20). John repeats this idea in Revelation 13:8, where he portrays Jesus as "the Lamb that was slain from the creation of the world." Together these verses tell us that God saves men and women not on the basis of their merits, good works, or anything else they have done. He saves humankind in accordance with His predetermined plan, His gracious election, the central focus of which is Jesus Christ. Believers are predestined only "in Christ," never apart from Christ.

2. *Historical.* What God decided and planned to do before the creation of the world, He has in fact actually accomplished in time and space. The drama of redemption unfolds throughout the Bible from the first messianic prophecy in Genesis 3:14-19, all the way through the Old Testament to the anguished cry of Golgotha, "My God, my God, why hast thou forsaken me?" (Matt. 27:46, KJV). On the cross Jesus bore the unmitigated penalty and damnation of sin and, standing in our place, satisfied the righteous demands of God's justice. "The Lord hath laid on him the iniquity of us all," Isaiah said in prophetic foresight (Isa. 53:6, KJV). The meaning of the cross, and its power too, were released by Jesus' resurrection from the dead, followed by His ascension back to heaven, and His pouring forth of the Holy Spirit on the Day of Pentecost. All of this is the result of God's grace, "his lavish gift-giving by the hand of his beloved Son" (Eph. 1:6, *The Message*).

Some people teach that God had devised a way of salvation for Old Testament saints based on law, and then came up with a different one for New Testament believers founded on grace. But this presents a serious misunderstanding of God's redemptive work. It is certainly true that Jesus was an incomparably greater king than Solomon, and that He promulgated an infinitely better covenant than Moses. But throughout history, God has had one and only one plan of salvation for everybody everywhere—by grace alone, through faith alone, in Jesus Christ alone! Old Testament saints saw only dimly and from afar what we now can look back upon and see clearly through the lenses of Calvary and Easter Sunday. But salvation was by grace for them no less than it is for us. In proclaiming this law-free gospel before the Council at Jerusalem, Peter declared that salvation was, as it always had been, by grace alone:

God has had one and only one plan of salvation for everybody everywhere—by grace, through faith in Jesus Christ!

Now then, why do you try to test God by putting on the necks of the disciples a yoke that neither we nor our fathers have been able to bear? No! We believe it is through the grace of our Lord Jesus that we are saved, just as they are (Acts 15:10-11).

3. Experiential. This refers to the personal, existential appropriation of Christ's redeeming work in the life of the believer. John Calvin put it this way: "As long as Christ remains outside of us, and we are separated from him, all that he has suffered and done for the salvation of the human race remains useless and of no value for us."[8] The experiential aspect of the economy of grace includes what the New

Testament calls our vocation or calling. This has both an outward and an inner dimension. These two are brought together in Ephesians 1:13. We are called externally through the faithful proclamation of the good news—"and you also were included in Christ when you heard the word of truth, the gospel of your salvation." Inwardly, we are called by the Holy Spirit who regenerates us (the new birth) as we repent of our sins and trust in Christ.

Having been justified and forgiven, Christians can live in the assurance that they are in a right standing with God, and that they will spend eternity with Him in heaven. Nicolaus von Zinzendorf, captured this note of Christian assurance in his hymn:

> Bold shall I stand in thy great day, For who aught to my charge shall lay? Fully absolved through these I am,
> From sin and fear, from guilt and shame.[9]

"Having believed, you were marked in him [Christ] with a seal, the promised Holy Spirit, who is a deposit guaranteeing our inheritance" (Eph. 1:13-14).

4. Eschatological. In his majestic overview of the operations of grace from eternity to eternity in Ephesians 1:3-14, Paul does not stop at the point of death, when the believer is united with Christ in heaven, nor even with the second coming of Christ. No, he looks beyond all of these great events to the final consummation of all things, to the moment when God's intended purpose in eternity past shall have been completely fulfilled. In the final consummation, "to bring all things in heaven and on earth together under one head, even Christ" (Eph. 1:10).

The Greek word for "to bring all things together" is *apokatastasis*, the longest word in the Greek New Testament. It refers to the ultimate wrapping up of human history, to God's cosmic victory over all the forces of evil. When this occurs everyone in the universe, not only Christians but also unbelievers who have died rejecting the love of Christ, together with the angels in heaven and the demons in hell, will exclaim together that Jesus Christ is Lord of lords and King of kings! And all of this is by grace too! What a great comfort to know that God's purpose will not be thwarted. In the meantime, all truly regenerated believers have been granted the gift of perseverance. We can celebrate our present and future security in the knowledge that, finally, every foe in heaven and on earth will be vanquished by the love of God. God will certainly complete the "good work" that He has begun in those He has redeemed (Phil. 1:6; see also 2:5-11).

All truly regenerated believers have been granted the gift of perseverance.

PERSONAL LEARNING ACTIVITY

Match the words in the left-hand column with the definitions in the right-hand column by drawing a line from each word to the correct definition.

Metahistorical	final consummation of all things
Historical	personal appropriation of Christ's redeeming work in the lives of believers
Experiential	God's purpose accomplished in time and space
Eschatological	before the world began

Grace in Depth

In this sweeping overview we have seen something of the "length and breadth" of God's dazzling, amazing grace as outlined in the Bible's story line from its origin in the eternal decrees through its final fulfillment at the end of time. This important perspective reminds us that grace is not an impersonal force or even a divine quality to be analyzed and studied abstractly. No, grace means God Himself is operating in love to the praise of His glory. As Martin Luther once said, "Grace is God's middle name!"

The New Testament states that Jesus "is also able to save to the uttermost those who come to God through Him" (Heb. 7:25, NKJV).

But at the heart of the gospel itself lies a "depth" dimension to grace. God's sufficient grace radiates its adequacy to meet the deepest needs of the vilest sinner who ever lived. There is no hell on earth so deep but that God's grace can go deeper still. Writers, such as Lewis Smedes, remind us that we experience grace on different levels in our lives including these:

• We experience grace as *pardon:* God's forgiveness and justification removes our guilty standing before Him, our real guilt not just our guilty feelings. The psalmist claims that God's pardoning grace removes our guilt of sin "as far as the east is from the west" (Ps. 103:12).

• We experience grace as *acceptance:* In Christ we who were distant from God, covered with shame, have been embraced, welcomed, and accepted—not because we are acceptable, but solely because we are loved.

• We experience grace as *joy:* This delivers us from the frantic quest to be "happy" by stuffing our lives with fleeting pleasures and "joyrides" which leave us sadder and more depressed. Real joy comes from knowing and serving God.

• We experience grace as *peace:* God's *shalom* answers the anxieties and insecurities which threaten us. The standard New Testament greeting is "grace and peace." Grace and peace are twins; they belong together, related as cause and effect.

• We experience grace as *power:* Most people do not so much lack the knowledge as they do the ability to carry out what they already know is right. God's grace acts as an antidote to our impotence. It transforms, energizes, empowers.

• We experience grace as *hope:* But not in the loose sense of a vague general wish which may not come true, as in "hopefully it won't rain tomorrow." In Titus 2:11-13, Paul connected the grace of God with the "blessed hope" of Jesus' return in glory, a great motivation for confident Christian living.

• We experience grace as *love:* God's grace and love are so close that, at times, we cannot distinguish them. God's gracious love counters all of our nagging fears and doubts.

• We experience grace as *gratitude:* The most basic response we can make to grace remains a life of "thank you's" to God. As Smedes points out, true gratitude involves "a sense of wonder and sometimes elation at the lavish generosity of God."[10] Later in this study, we will look at the way grace has been understood throughout the history of the church, including some of the controversies it has generated among believers through the ages. But we must never forget that, first and foremost, grace is not something to be studied, analyzed, and argued about; rather it is something to be received and experienced, by which we are changed.

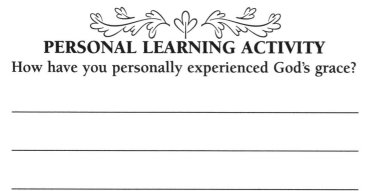

PERSONAL LEARNING ACTIVITY
How have you personally experienced God's grace?

_____

_____

_____

The Bible says that "perfect love casts out fear" (1 John 4:18, NKJV).

---

[1] Julia H. Johnston, "Grace Greater than Our Sin," Stanza 3.

[2] "Room at the Cross for You" by Ira F. Stanphill, ©1946 Singspiration Music (ASCAP), a division of Brentwood-Benson Music Publishing, Inc. All rights reserved. Used by permission.

[3] Alexander Roberts and James Donaldson, eds., *The Ante-Nicene Fathers: Translations of The Writings of the Fathers down to A.D. 325* (Grand Rapids, Mich.:WM. B. Eerdmans Publishing Company, 1980), 46.

[4] Arthur C. McGill, *Suffering: A Test of Theological Method* (Philadelphia, Penn.: The Geneva Press, 1968), 64.

[5] Karl Barth, *Dogmatics in Outline* (New York: Harper & Row Publishers, 1959), 54.

[6] Thomas Hardy, *The Dynasts, Part 3* (London: MacMillan and Co., 1913), 254.

[7] Oscar Hardman, *The Christian Doctrine of Grace* (New York: The MacMillan Company, 1947), 9.

[8] John T. McNeill, ed., *Calvin: Institutes of the Christian Religion,* vol. XX, (Philadelphia, Penn.: The Westminster Press, 1960), 537.

[9] Nicolaus von Zinzendorf, "Jesus, Thy Blood and Righteousness," Stanza 2.

[10] Lewis B. Smedes, *Shame and Grace* (New York: HarperCollins Publishers, 1993), 108.

CHAPTER TWO

The Providence Mystery

There are many things Christians believe simply because they are undeniably taught in the Bible. Yet we cannot remove all questions and puzzlements. We cannot explain with precision how these things can be true in terms of human reason and logic. Consider the doctrine of the Holy Trinity. Orthodox Christians of all confessions believe in the Trinity. We believe that the one true God is, and from all eternity has ever been, the Father, the Son, and the Holy Spirit. Yet, we ask, how can God be One and Three at the same time? Or, consider the fact of the Incarnation. Nothing is more central to the gospel itself than John 1:14: "The Word became flesh and made his dwelling among us." It's a stupendous thought—the Creator of heaven and earth tethered to a human umbilical cord! How can this be, we wonder? How do we explain that Jesus was fully divine, "very God of very God," as the ancient confession declares,[2] and yet at the same time completely human with genes, chromosomes and DNA molecules of His own, with eyes that cried real tears and toes that turned blue when He stubbed them?

Or, how about this: We believe that God is absolutely sovereign over all that He has made. And we also believe that He has given free moral agency and responsibility to the men and women created in His image. How can this be? Keep this question in mind as we examine what the Bible teaches about the providence of God—the way God sustains and governs the world and moves it along, guiding it moment by moment, toward its appointed end.

Before we consider the question of providence, let's look at four words which are often used when we ponder the difficult questions that baffle the human mind, issues such as the Trinity, or Christology, or the relationship between predestination and human freedom.

• **The first is contradiction:** A contradiction refers to a condition in which at least two things are at variance, that is, truly contrary to each other. A real contradiction involves a genuine discrepancy, not merely an apparent inconsistency. In the garden of Eden, God told Adam and Eve that death would be the penalty for eating the forbidden fruit. When Satan said, "You will not surely die," he contradicted God (Gen. 3:4).

• **The second is antinomy:** An antinomy is a combination of two thoughts or principles, each of which is true in its own right but which we cannot harmonize. J.I. Packer uses the example of light as an antinomy in physics. Does light consist of waves or particles, he asks? Good evidence supports both views and both must be treated as true, even though they seem incompatible to our understanding of the universe.

• **The third is paradox:** Close to the meaning of antinomy, it is sometimes used as synonymous with it, but there is an important distinction. Some scholars believe a paradox (from the Greek *para,* beyond, and *doxa,* opinion or belief) appears to be a contradiction. It seems to be something absurd, but, when we look closer, it proves to be true, in fact. For example when Paul says, "When I am weak, then I am strong" (2 Cor. 12:10), he is speaking paradoxically for his words are quite comprehensible, though still jarring once we understand his intended use of them.

• **The fourth is mystery:** Mystery refers to a whole complex of ideas including antinomies and paradoxes that we know on good grounds to be true, but is inexplicable or inscrutable. Mystery means something which has been kept secret. In theology, a mystery is a truth which the human mind cannot comprehend, but which we must accept by faith.

Christians are those who have already glimpsed something of the unfathomable "mystery" of God's will in Christ (Eph. 1:9; see also Rom. 16:25-27), as we have seen in Paul's depiction of God's great purpose of grace. By His mercy and grace, God has let us in on His secret plan. And yet there is much that we do not know. We don't yet see "face to face," but only partially, dimly. Sometimes life seems like a jigsaw puzzle

Christians have already glimpsed something of the unfathomable "mystery" of God's will in Christ.

"For in this hope we were saved. But hope that is seen is no hope at all. Who hopes for what he already has? But if we hope for what we do not yet have, we wait for it patiently" (Rom. 8:24-25).

with some of the pieces missing. "At present we are looking at puzzling reflections in a mirror … at present all I know is a little fraction of the truth" (1 Cor. 13:12, *Phillips*). For this reason Christians walk through life by faith, not by sight. Only God is omniscient. We know some things surely, but we don't know everything for sure. We have been saved, and yet we still suffer. We live in hope for we are not exempt from the "groanings" of the fallen world around us.

PERSONAL LEARNING ACTIVITY

Four words are used to consider difficult biblical questions: (1) contradiction, (2) antimony, (3) paradox, and (4) mystery. In the blanks below, write the number of the word that corresponds to the definition of that word.

____ combination of two thoughts or principles, each of which is true, but which cannot be harmonized in our own minds

____ condition in which two things are at variance

____ assumed truth which the mind cannot comprehend, but which we must accept by faith

____ apparent contradiction that when closely examined proves to be true

The Doctrine of Providence

What is divine providence? Let's look at two classic definitions of providence from the Baptist heritage. The first comes from a 17th-century confession of faith called "The Orthodox Creed," published by General or Arminian Baptists in 1679:

The Almighty God that created all things and gave them their being by His infinite power and wisdom, doth sustain and uphold and move, direct, dispose, and govern all creatures and things from the greatest to the least, according to the counsel of His own good will and pleasure, for His own glory and His creatures, good.[3]

The second definition comes from the first confessional statement published by Southern Baptists after the founding of the Southern Baptist Convention in 1845. We call this the "Abstract of Principles." It is still used as the primary doctrinal standard (and subscribed by all professors) in two of the denomination's seminaries:

God from eternity, decrees or permits all things that come to pass, and perpetually upholds, directs and governs all creatures and all events; yet so as not in any wise to be the author or approver of sin nor to destroy the free will and responsibility of intelligent creatures.[4]

These quotations show that, despite their different understandings about some matters (such as predestination and the possibility of losing one's salvation), Baptists with both Arminian and Calvinistic leanings are largely agreed in their teaching about divine providence. We can summarize the general thrust of these two statements in three affirmations:

1. Nothing exists except in some relationship to God.
At the heart of biblical faith stands the doctrine of creation "out of nothing" (*ex nihilo* in Latin). God didn't make the world out of some kind of primordial matter, matter that already existed. Plato depicted him doing this in the *Timaeus*: an Artisan shaping the world out of a kind of cosmic modeling clay. This is not the biblical view of creation. No, God spoke, and things that did not previously exist came into being. Every molecule or atom in the universe owes its origin to the sovereign Lord of time and eternity. The 24 elders in heaven acknowledge this truth when they sing:

Creation is at the heart of biblical faith.

You are worthy, our Lord and God, to receive glory and honor
and power, for you created all things,
And by your will they existed and were created (Rev. 4:11).

God created all things. Heaven, too, is a created place, along with the angels and other heavenly beings. The prayer of Ezra in Nehemiah 9:6 clearly connects creation and providence:

You are the Lord, you alone; you have made heaven, the heaven
of heavens, with all their hosts, the earth and all that is on it,
the seas and all that is in them; and you preserve all of them;
and the host of heaven worships you.

Although it may seem to us that things happen by chance or accident, there are no accidents, so far as God's purpose is concerned.

As Dale Moody put it: "Belief in God as creator denies self-existence to things. Things are dependent upon God not only in their origin but also in their continuation and consummation. The action of God in the continuation of creation is his work of preservation."[5]

2. *Nothing happens apart from God's purposeful activity.* When the "Abstract of Principles" declares that God "decrees or permits all things that come to pass," it simply echoes the clear teaching of the Bible. The Psalms are filled with affirmations of God's comprehensive providence: "The Lord has established his throne in heaven, and his kingdom rules over all" (Ps. 103:19). And again, "I know that the Lord is great, that our Lord is greater than all gods. The Lord does whatever pleases him, in the heavens and on the earth, in the seas and all their depths. He makes clouds rise from the ends of the earth; he sends lightning with the rain and brings out the wind from his storehouses" (Ps. 135:5-7). To us, it might seem that things happen by chance, at random. "Oh, that was an accident," we say. But there are no accidents with God. Even events like rolling dice or flipping coins are ordered by Him, as Proverbs 16:33 makes clear: "The lot is cast into the lap, but its every decision is from the Lord." This is why Paul can state so boldly that God "works *all things* according to the counsel of His will" (Eph. 1:11, NKJV).

3. Nothing can thwart God's gracious design in Christ. We can not think of providence apart from Jesus Christ. Through Him, God made everything in heaven and on earth (see John 1:3). He continually upholds the universe by the power of His word (see Heb. 1:3). Jesus remains the eternal divine agent in both creation and providence: "In him," Paul said, "all things hold together" (Col. 1:17). God has "put all things in subjection under his feet" (Heb. 2:8, NKJV) and, amidst all the ambiguities of history, He is guiding the world and everything within it toward its divinely appointed end. So that ultimately "Jesus Christ is Lord" will be on the lips of every sentient being from heaven down to hell (Phil. 2:5-10).

PERSONAL LEARNING ACTIVITY
Confessional statements from both the 17th and 19th centuries may be summarized in these statements:

1. **Nothing exists apart from God.**
2. **Nothing happens apart from God's purposeful activity**
3. **Nothing can thwart God's gracious design in Christ.**

   Which one of the affirmations is most meaningful to you? Why?

_____

_____

Intervening and Interweaving
This is a sweeping view of God as the sovereign disposer of all that is—a theology of God without any loose ends. No honest reading of the Bible allows anything else, and we have sampled only a fraction of the thousands of passages that

A biblical theology of God has no loose ends.

The God of the Bible is not a God of brute force or arrogant self-will.

underscore this truth. But, we ask, does such a view leave enough "elbow room" for meaningful human participation within the orders of creation? Doesn't God's sovereignty and providence devour human responsibility and undercut all morality?

At this point let's review everything said in chapter 1 about the gracious character of God. God is omnipotent and all-powerful. He is also omnibenevolent, all-loving. *God is love*—love is His very essence. We will return to this theme when we look at the difference between the biblical view of God's providential governance and various forms of fatalism or determinism. The God of the Bible is not a God of brute force or arrogant self-will. This is a better definition of the devil, for it was Satan who continued to say, "I will ... I will ... I will" (Isa. 14:12-15). No, the God of the covenant, the God whom Jesus taught us to call *Abba,* is kind and generous. In His utter holiness, He is a God of never-failing mercy and compassion. We are amazed at His forbearance, at His extravagant grace and inexpressible love. Can we do anything less than say with the children of Israel: "Give thanks to the Lord, for he is good. His love endures forever" (Ps. 136:1)? We must keep this in mind when we acknowledge that "God's works of providence are his most holy, wise, and powerful preserving and governing all his creatures, and all their actions."[6]

The Bible undoubtedly teaches divine sovereignty—but that is only one side of the antinomy. It also makes room for human freedom and accountability. Psalm 47:2: "For the Lord Most High is awesome; He is a great King over all the earth" (NKJV) is answered by Psalm 138:6: "Though the Lord is on high, he looks upon the lowly." Just as many Bible texts teach human responsibility as those that teach divine sovereignty. Again and again through the prophets, God pleaded for His people to repent, to turn from their wicked ways, and to seek His face. Many times the children of Israel were confronted with words such as these: "The Lord is with you when you are with him. If you seek him, he will be found by you, but if you forsake him, he will forsake you" (2 Chron. 15:2). God may have hardened Pharaoh's heart, but even that wicked ruler was not an unthinking puppet. Far from it—he was a malicious evildoer whom God holds accountable. In the New Testament, Jesus wept over the city of Jerusalem and exclaimed, "How often I have longed to gather your children together, as a hen gathers her chicks under her wings, *but you were not willing!*" (Luke 13:34, emphasis added). The sin and rejection of Jerusalem's people could not thwart Christ's saving mission, but their free moral agency was not extinguished by Jesus' march to Calvary. Their choice to spurn the Savior's love was tragically all too real.

Granted, the Bible affirms both God's sovereignty and human free agency in the course of events. But how is it that God accomplishes His providential purposes within the world? The answer is twofold: Sometimes by *intervening* directly, immediately, miraculously. More often, though, by *interweaving* His guidance and rule with the intentions and freely chosen acts of human beings. Numerous examples of God's radical intervention in the lives of His people and in the course of nature fill the Bible. He sent the flood as an expression of His judgment. He visited Egypt with plagues and rescued Israel from the clutches of Pharaoh "with a mighty hand" (Deut. 7:8). He smote the army of the Assyrians leaving many thousands dead. He healed the sick and raised the dead. He engineered Peter's miraculous escape from prison and rescued Jonah from a seafaring death. When God acts in such a swift and unilateral way we stand amazed.

But even more frequently, we see the hand of God in the interlacing of divine and human activity. After years of languishing in exile, God allowed the children of Israel to return to their homeland through the intervention of Cyrus, the ruler of Persia. Their release was Cyrus's idea; under no compulsion or constraint, he freely chose to liberate the Israelites and send them home. Yet when the prophet Isaiah considered this momentous event, he ascribed it to God: "Who has done this and carried it through? ... I, the Lord ... I am he" (Isa. 41:4). Clearly God worked through Cyrus. We

Moses and the children of Israel sang of the intervening hand of God in the Exodus: "Who among the gods is like you, O Lord? Who is like you—majestic in holiness, awesome in glory, working wonders?" (Ex. 15:11).

can even say that God used Cyrus, including his freely chosen decisions to accomplish what God had intended (and promised) to do beforehand.

The death of Christ is another example of how God's providence works in and through freely chosen human acts. Jesus was the Lamb of God who was slain from the foundation of the world. The shadow of the cross fell over every event of His life from Bethlehem to Calvary. For centuries the prophets had predicted the sacrificial atoning death of the Messiah, as Jesus Himself acknowledged, "Did not the Christ have to suffer these things and then enter his glory?" (Luke 24:26). Clearly Jesus was put to death at the hands of cruel men who tortured and crucified Him outside the gates of Jerusalem. The crucifiers were not marionettes dancing on a string. They were free moral agents fully accountable for their heinous deeds. Peter made this clear in his sermon on the Day of Pentecost: "This man was handed over to you by God's set purpose and foreknowledge; and you, with the help of wicked men, put him to death by nailing him to the cross" (Acts 2:23). In the same verse, Peter attributes the one event of Jesus' death to two centers of intentionality: God's set purpose and the hands of wicked men. This motif was so pervasive among the earliest Christians that they incorporated it into their prayer life:

> *Indeed Herod and Pontius Pilate met together with the Gentiles and the people of Israel in this city to conspire against your holy servant Jesus, whom you anointed.* They did what your power and will had decided beforehand should happen
> (*Acts 4:27-28, emphasis added*).

You [God] had *decided* ... and they *did!*

Note carefully the Bible never explains *how* the sinful acts of wicked men coalesce with God's sovereign purpose, but somehow mysteriously they do work together concurrently. G.K. Chesterton observed that "Christianity got over the difficulty of combining furious opposites, by keeping them

> The cross of Christ is an example of how God's providence works in and through freely chosen human acts.

both, and keeping them both furious."[7] Our finite human minds cannot comprehend such an antinomy. We are tempted to resolve it either by qualifying God's sovereignty or by denying human free agency. While this solution is neater logically, it could never be acceptable biblically. To be faithful to what God has revealed about how He works in the affairs of this world, we must say both/and, not either/or.

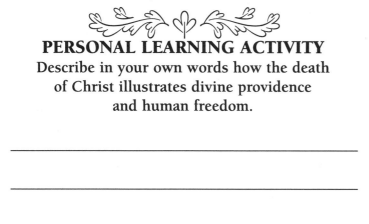

PERSONAL LEARNING ACTIVITY
Describe in your own words how the death
of Christ illustrates divine providence
and human freedom.

_____

_____

_____

Four Dead Ends

We must distinguish the biblical view of providence from several competing perspectives which, however popular in some circles, do not square with the evidence of Scripture.

• *Deism:* Deists believe that God, having constructed the world in the beginning, has since then left it to run its course more or less on its own. The god of deism is high and mighty, transcendent and aloof, but he is also distant and removed from the daily goings-on of everyday life. Deism denies to God what the Bible everywhere attributes—a watchful, effective, active, ceaseless engagement with the governance of the world He has created. Deism de-personalizes God. It gives us omnipotence without the Almighty, sovereignty apart from the Sovereign. No wonder that deism has become for many a way station on the road to atheism! If God is seen merely as the First Cause, the Final Force, or the Cosmic Glue that holds it all together, then He can be quite easily dispensed within the

The Bible does not support the false idea that God created the world, then left it on its own to run its course.

interest of secular naturalism. Today deism as a system of thought is a spent force, but, as Wayne Grudem has noted "many … nominal Christians today are, in effect, practical deists, since they live lives almost totally devoid of genuine prayer, worship, fear of God, or moment-by-moment trust in God to care for needs that arise."[8]

• *Pantheism:* This stands at the opposite extreme from deism. It equates God and the created order by claiming that God is everything and everything is God. Deism makes God transcendent and removes Him far away from the affairs of daily life. Pantheism makes God utterly immanent, collapsing all distinction between the Creator and the creature. God is no longer personal in any sense, but merely the manifestation of all laws, forces, and principles of the self-existing universe. Today's New Age spirituality shows a strong pantheistic current when its "believers" worship nature, the earth, the cosmos, or "the god within."

• *Fatalism:* The biblical doctrine of providence is vastly different from a heartless determinism or fatalism. Fatalism teaches that everything is entirely determined by an inviolable sequence of cause and effect. Thus every event we "choose" to do—from casting a vote to brushing our teeth—is not free, but determined by a sequence of causes independent of our own wills. Some forms of fatalism teach that human destiny is linked with the stars. This is why so many people read the daily horoscope with religious fervor hoping to discover the secret to romance or riches. Among the world religions, Islam is known for its necessitarian theology (events proceed from causes), while atheistic determinism undergirds many modern approaches to human life, such as behaviorist psychology and Freudian psychoanalysis. But the Bible never presents God's providence as a scheme of strict determinism. God "makes room" for the creatures He has made in His own image. He endows them with creaturely freedom, even though He knows in advance that they will misuse it to their own detriment. As the "Abstract of Principles" puts it, God never destroys "the free will and responsibility of intelligent creatures." On the

> The God of the Bible is more than a manifestation of the laws, forces, and principles of His creation.

contrary God works *in* and *through* all freely chosen human decisions, including quite horrible ones such as the decision of Pilate and the Jewish religious leaders to crucify Jesus, as a means to accomplish the redemptive purpose He has planned from all eternity.

G.C. Berkouwer explains the difference between the Christian view of providence and deterministic fatalism:

> Divine determining is utterly different from what is generally understood by determinism. It is not that there is a material similarity between the confession of God's Providence and determinism and that the only difference between them is the formal difference that in determinism the first cause stands at the end of the series of causes, while in the confession of Providence *God* stands there. Since we have to do with the Providence of *God,* everything else, including planning, determining, and acting, is different. This is why we never find in the Scriptures either the rigidity or the violence typical of determinism. In the confession of God's almighty power, the personal, living God is confessed. Responsibility is not crowded out by His power; neither is the meaning of guilt and punishment. We are deeply conscious of the impossibility of our discerning the relation between the Divine activity and ours, but we are able to see in Scripture that the incomparable enterprise of God is in its Divine character so great and majestic that it can embrace human freedom and responsibility within itself without being thereby assaulted or even limited.[9]

• *Process Theism:* In its starkest form, process theism denies the sovereignty of God by positioning another reality alongside God by which He is necessarily limited—matter perhaps, or the universe, or chaos. A somewhat softer form of process thinking has gained currency in recent years under the banner of "the openness of God." This view denies that

God is not limited by any opposing reality in the universe.

God is Lord of all creation and all events, including the future.

God has exhaustive knowledge of the future, because, so the theory runs, the future is not really "there" to be known even by God! While pretending to "protect" God against a false view of sovereignty that would exclude Him from meaningful interaction within the realm of space and time, this so-called "open" view of God actually reduces Him to the creaturely level by closing off both the reality of predictive prophecy and the urgency of petitionary prayer. Process theology, in all its forms, remains a dangerous deviation from historic Christian orthodoxy. It has been repudiated, through the centuries, by Calvinists, Arminians, Protestants, and Catholics.

PERSONAL LEARNING ACTIVITY
Mark the following statements as true or false.

___ Professing Christians who live life devoid of genuine prayer, worship, fear of God, or moment-by-moment trust in God are practical deists.

___ Pantheism claims that God is everything and everything is God.

___ Fatalism and the biblical doctrine of providence are strikingly similar in definition.

___ Process theism is an attempt to limit God.

Lessons from Providence

Meditation on the ways of God serves as an important spiritual discipline in the lives of Christians. It is a mark of Christian maturity to confess with the psalmist that "the Lord is righteous in all his ways, and holy in all his works" (Ps. 145:17, KJV). We must be aware of false perspectives and theological dead ends lest we be robbed of the great comfort God has for us in the doctrine of providence. Our consideration of this theme, however, is not a matter of philosophical speculation or theological argument. Our faith should be strengthened as we consider how our lives are governed by the wisdom and care of our loving Heavenly Father. As J.B. Phillips translates Romans 8:28: "We know that to those who love God, who are called according to his plan, everything that happens fits into a pattern for good." We can learn many things from the study of providence, including these five principles:

1. The doctrine of providence reminds us that God is the sovereign Lord of history. The God of the Bible is a "hands-on" God, intimately concerned with the smallest details of our lives. But He is also the Creator and Judge of the world which He is infallibly guiding toward its predestined goal. Theologians sometimes distinguish God's *special providence* (which relates to the salvation and care of His chosen people) from God's *general providence* (which is comparable to common grace), through which He governs the courses of nature and history. This is a helpful distinction in some ways, but we should not press it too far. As we saw in the example of Cyrus, secular and sacred are mysteriously intermingled in the unfolding drama of redemption. God used the events of so-called secular history to prepare the way for the coming of Christ, who was born in the fullness of time (see Gal. 4:4). And He still sustains and guides the church through all the ups and downs of historical change and conflict.

Textbooks on history often read as though politics and economics are the decisive determiners in the course of history: wars are won by those who have the best diplomats or the biggest bombs; prosperity hinges on this or that economic system. The Bible, however, tells us that another hidden, often invisible, factor needs to be considered: the hand of God. As Daniel 5:21 puts it, "The Most High God is sovereign over the kingdoms of men and sets over them anyone he wishes." Again, Proverbs 21:1 says, "The king's heart is in the hand of the Lord; he directs it like a watercourse wherever he pleases." God sometimes even uses evil and

The God of the Bible is a "hands-on" God, who is intimately concerned with the smallest details of our lives.

tyrannical powers to accomplish His purposes. The rise and fall of nations and empires does not happen apart from God's superintendence: "God is the Judge: He puts down one, And exalts another" (Ps. 75:7, NKJV).

Because God is the Lord of history, Christians must not give unqualified allegiance to any earthly power or political regime. Of course, we should love our country and pray for our leaders, but let us be wary of equating political success with divine favor. In the 1930s, many German Christians forgot this principle. Swept along in the rising tide of Nazism, a group of German theologians made this statement in 1934: "We are full of thanks to God that He, as Lord of history, has given us Adolf Hitler, our leader and savior from our difficult lot. We acknowledge that we, with body and soul, are bound and dedicated to the German state and to its *Fuhrer.*"[10]

How different was the witness of Martin Niemöller, a Lutheran pastor imprisoned by the Gestapo for his opposition to the Nazi state. On one occasion, when he was being ridiculed and taunted by Hitler himself, he reminded the dictator, in the words of Jesus before Pilate, you have no authority except what God has given to you, and one day things will look different when both of us stand before the bar of God's judgment. Today, when many Christians are still persecuted for their faith, it is a great comfort to know that God's cause is not in doubt. His purpose of grace will triumph over Satan and all his pomp.

2. We often see the pattern of providence only in retrospect. William Cowper's great hymn on providence, "God Moves in a Mysterious Way," contains these lines:

Judge not the Lord by feeble sense, But trust Him for His grace;
   Behind a frowning providence He hides a smiling face.

Blind unbelief is sure to err And scan His work in vain;
   God is His own interpreter, And He will make it plain.[11]

The "making plain" part baffles many Christians. When we are

> **Christians should be wary of equating political power with divine favor.**

overcome by grief or confronted with a tragic event either in our own lives or that of a loved one, we seldom see how these experiences fit into God's plan for us. But when we look back over our lives from the perspective of, say, five years, or ten, or twenty or more, we can understand more clearly some of those things that at the time brought only tears and questions.

Remember the biblical story of Joseph? On one level it is a simple plot. Mean brothers betray a spoiled-brat kid. They send him to a foreign country as a slave. There, after being falsely accused of a crime he did not commit, he goes to prison with no hope of release. Surely, from the pit and then the prison, Joseph must have wondered about the goodness of a God who could have allowed such things to happen to him. *Why me? Why has this happened to me?* He could see no purpose in these events. But later on, when he disclosed his true identity to his brothers, he made an astonishing statement: "It was not you who sent me here, but God. ... You intended to harm me but God intended it for good to accomplish what is now being done, the saving of many lives" (Gen. 45:8; 50:20). Note carefully: Not only did God permit what occurred to come to pass, but also He actually *intended* it. He "meant" it, as the *King James Version* states it. What Joseph's brothers did, of course, was wicked in every respect; they were not absolved of responsibility for their treachery. But God in His sovereignty was also at work even in that horrible circumstance to accomplish something marvelous. Joseph realized this only in retrospect. By looking back he saw the pattern of God's providence in his life and those of his brothers as well. God intended it for good not only for Joseph and his brothers, but also for the whole world. Through the survival of Joseph's family an entire nation would emerge— and from this nation the Messiah would be born.

3. God uses suffering and tragedy as occasions to display His glory. In the face of suffering and tragedy, we can either deny God's ability to prevent the disaster, and consequently think of God as impotent in the face of radical evil, or, more commonly, we can blame God for not intervening. When a

Someday we will understand how events we do not understand at the present time fit into God's loving purpose.

Behind our suffering, we trust the one God who ever remains a wise and loving Father who has promised never to leave or forsake us.

fellow minister lost his young daughter to cancer, a well-known pastor tried to comfort him by saying: "God will have a lot to give account for in heaven." No one can deny these feelings when faced with such a crisis. The Bible itself, especially the Psalms, overflows with questions born of pain and doubt: "How long, O Lord? ... How long will you hide your face from me?" (Ps. 13:1); "Why, O Lord, do you stand far off?" (Ps. 10:1). But true piety knows that, behind the suffering, we experience the one God who ever remains in His justice, a wise and loving Father who has promised never to leave or forsake us. When we charge God with complicity in evil, we assume that God and humans are subject to the same standards of judgment. That's like comparing apples and oranges, or asking how many inches are in a pound. What God said through the prophet Isaiah still stands: "'For my thoughts are not your thoughts, neither are your ways my ways,' declares the Lord. 'As the heavens are higher than the earth, so are my ways higher than your ways and my thoughts than your thoughts'" (Isa. 55:8-9).

The Bible spends little time answering the why's and wherefore's of life. Rather, it tells us that "the secret things belong to the Lord our God, but the things revealed belong to us and to our children forever" (Deut. 29:29). When confronted with a man born blind (see John 9), Jesus refused to talk about the cause of his blindness. He does say that the blindness was not caused by his sin or his parents' sin. Jesus focused not on causation, but on purpose: "this happened so that the work of God might be displayed in his life" (v. 3). His blindness became the occasion for God's grace because God healed him physically and spiritually, and he became an effective witness to the saving power of Christ.

4. God's grace is sufficient when the answer is "no." Second Corinthians 12:7-10 is one of the Bible's most important passages on the role of providence in the Christian life. Paul told us he had a debilitating physical ailment: "a thorn in my flesh." We do not know what this "thorn" meant (some have guessed blindness or epilepsy), but Paul told us four important things about it. First, God "gave" it to him for his spiritual well-being—to keep him from arrogance and pride. Second, the devil had a hand in it: He was tormented by "a messenger of Satan." This recalls the same way God allowed Satan to afflict Job in the Old Testament. Third, Paul repeatedly prayed for relief, but God answered him with "no." Finally, through this experience Paul drew closer to Christ. He came to know more deeply the sufficiency of God's grace. At the end of the experience he said: "Now I take limitations in stride, and with good cheer, these limitations that cut me down to size—abuse, accidents, opposition, bad breaks. I just let Christ take over! And so the weaker I get, the stronger I become" (2 Cor. 12:10, *The Message*).

I shall never forget Sue McIntyre. She was the wife of the pastor, Dr. J. Ralph McIntyre, who ordained me to the gospel ministry. Sue was one of the godliest women I have ever known. She radiated the love of Jesus in everything she did. She was a great encouragement to me and to the other young people in the church. Soon after I moved to Boston to begin graduate studies, I learned that Sue had been diagnosed with cancer. She struggled for several years but then died in the prime of life. I was not able to come home for the funeral, but someone sent me a tape of the service. I remember listening to the voice of her husband as he delivered the message at her funeral. He said that if he could snap his fingers and change the course of events, he would do so in a second for he deeply loved his "sweet Sue" [as he called her]. But then he went on to say that he was not angry with God. He and Sue had talked together before she died. Even though they had many questions neither one could answer, they both found God's grace completely sufficient for the valley they were walking through together. And this has been the testimony of countless Christians through the ages: "When all around, my soul gives way, He then is all my hope and stay."[12]

5. The cross is the place where grace and providence embrace. Where can we look to find confirmation of Romans 8:28—to know that God's work of grace will finally triumph

God's grace is completely sufficient for the valleys through which we walk.

43

over all obstacles? We can see some evidence of this in our own lives, especially as we review them retrospectively through the lens of God's redemptive love. Sometimes we can see what appears to be God's movement on a grand scale in history—as with the fall of Communism in recent years. But these perspectives are always partial, always incomplete. We are still looking into a mirror with blurred vision. We can look one place, however, and know beyond all doubt that Romans 8:28 is true: the cross of our Lord Jesus Christ. We call it Good Friday, but it proved to be one of the darkest days in history. Abandoned by His followers and friends, a crucified Jesus experienced a God-forsaken death for God-forsaken sinners. Amazingly, when Christians looked back on this event, they saw not defeat but triumph, for God was in Christ reconciling the world unto Himself on that cross. Thus in an ancient Syrian liturgy, the early Christians sang, "The Lord hath reigned from the tree."[13] God used the innocent, shameful, despicable suffering of His own Son to bring about the eternal good of redemption. We can be sure He also will take the shards and broken fragments in our lives and piece them together into a mosaic of beauty and wonder. The God who neither slumbers nor sleeps will see us through the darkest night and bring us safe at last to that blessed place where we will need neither lamp nor light of sun. God Himself will be our radiance. What a great comfort! What a great God of majesty and wonder, worthy of worship and praise, as Isaac Watts knew when he wrote this hymn:

> Tell of His wondrous faithfulness, And sound His power
> abroad; Sing the sweet promise of His grace,
> And the performing God.

> Engraved as in eternal brass, The mighty promise shines;
> Nor can the powers of darkness rase Those everlasting lines.

> His very word of grace is strong As that which built the skies;
> The voice that rolls the stars along Speaks all the promises.[14]

When Christians look back to the cross, they see not defeat but triumph, for God was in Christ reconciling the world unto Himself.

PERSONAL LEARNING ACTIVITY

Five principles may be learned from the study of
Providence. One of these is "God uses suffering
and tragedy as occasions to display His glory."
How has this principle impacted your life?

_____

_____

**Can one grow through tragedy and suffering?
Please explain below.**

_____

_____

[1] John Flavel, *The Mystery of Providence* (Edinburgh: The Banner of Truth Trust, 1678), 15.

[2] n.a., *The Constitution of the Presbyterian Church (U.S.A.): Part I—Book of Confessions* (New York: The Office of the General Assembly, 1983), 1.1-3.

[3] John Broadus, Timothy and Denise George, eds., *Baptist Confessions, Covenants, and Catechisms* (Nashville, Tenn., Broadman & Holman Publishers, 1996), 101-102. ©1996 by Broadman & Holman. Used by permission.

[4] Robert A. Baker, *A Baptist Source Book* (Nashville, Tenn.: Broadman Press, 1966), 138. Copyright 1966. Renewed 1994 Broadman Press. All rights reserved. Used by permission.

[5] Dale Moody, *The Word of Truth* (Grand Rapids, Mich.: William B. Eerdmans Publishing Company, 1981), 137.

[6] *The Constitution of the Presbyterian Church (U.S.A.),* 7.011.

[7] Gilbert K. Chesterton, *Orthodoxy* (New York: John Lane Company, 1908), 174.

[8] Wayne Grudem, *Systematic Theology* (Leicester, England: InterVarsity Press, and Grand Rapids, Mich.: Zondervan Publishing House, 1994), 270-271.

[9] G.C. Berkouwer, *The Providence of God* (Grand Rapids, Mich.: William B. Eerdmans Publishing Company, 1952), 151-152.

[10] Berkouwer, 162.

[11] William Cowper, "God Moves in a Mysterious Way."

[12] Edward Mote, "The Solid Rock."

[13] Carlyle Marney, *The Crucible of Redemption* (Wake Forest, N.C.: Chanticleer Publishing Company, Inc., 1968), 62.

[14] Isaac Watts, "The Triune God."

CHAPTER THREE

Saved by Grace

On our feet we may have arguments about it, but on our knees we are all agreed.[1]
J.I. Packer

Recently I received a package of Ginseng-flavored tea as a present. As I opened the box, I noticed the following verse, entitled "Determination," inscribed on the back:

> Gifts count for nothing; will alone is great; All things give way before it, soon or late. ... Each well-born soul must win what it deserves. ... The fortunate Is he whose earnest purpose never swerves, Whose slightest action or inaction serves The one great aim. Why, even Death stands still, And waits an hour sometimes for such a will.[2]

Since Adam and Eve fell in the garden of Eden, the following sentiments have been the creed of graceless human beings. Gifts count for nothing. What does count is your will, your determination. You can make it on your own. Grace is for weaklings. You need no Savior to die for you, because you can save yourself by what you do and how you live. Just dig in deeper, and try harder! William Ernest Henley's famous poem, "Invictus" expresses the same idea in its exaltation of "my unconquerable soul. ... I am the master of my fate: I am the captain of my soul."[3]

Yet anyone who has been born again knows that this cannot be right. Self-salvation is an impossibility. Life itself is a gift. Moment by moment we are sustained by God's gracious providence. Everything we are and have is the result of our dependence on God's mercy. Sometimes, though, we have to be brought low before we realize this basic truth. Jonah had spent some time in the belly of the fish before he was ready to confess, "Salvation is of the Lord" (Jonah 2:9, KJV).

Occasionally when I am speaking at a church or Bible conference, some young person will ask me to sign his or her Bible. When I do, I always include a reference to my favorite

Bible verse: 1 Corinthians 4:7. This verse shatters the myth of self-reliance and points us to the reality of salvation by grace better than any text I know. It consists of three questions:

1. Who makes you different from anyone else?
2. What do you have that you did not receive?
3. And if you did receive it, why do you boast as though you did not?

When they reflect on it, all Christians know that God did not save them because they are better, or smarter, or nicer looking than anyone else. In the Old Testament, God reminded the children of Israel that He had not chosen them because they were large in number, or mighty in battle, or rich in resources. No, they were at the very bottom of "the most favored nation" list. Why then, did God choose Israel? Because of His unmerited favor. He loved them—just because! And what can any of us claim to have, to possess, that we have not received as a gift? The honest answer has to be … nothing. The air we breathe, the clothes we wear, the food we eat, our families, our jobs, our friends, our faith: all of this has come to us as a gift from our gracious God (see Jas. 1:17). Because this is true, there is no basis for boasting in the Christian life, no room for one-upmanship in the family of God. In the realm of grace, we lose all our bragging rights. Here we can only glory "in the cross of our Lord Jesus Christ" (Gal. 6:14).

The Bible could not be more emphatic that salvation is a free gift of God. As Paul put it: "There is no distinction; for all have sinned and fall short of the glory of God, being justified as a gift by His grace through the redemption which is in Christ Jesus" (Rom. 3:22-24, NASB). And yet the doctrine of grace has been the subject of continual controversy throughout the history of the church. Why is this? Partly because the grace of God, for all its simplicity, is a difficult teaching to accept. There is a natural resistance to the extravagance of grace. Like the prodigal son returning from the far country, we think we must "do something" to earn the Father's favor. But there is another reason for the controversy as well. Like the

Christians know that God did not save them because they are better, or smarter, or nicer looking than anyone else.

mystery of providence, the doctrine of salvation by grace alone raises difficult questions about divine sovereignty and human responsibility, about predestination and the universal love of God. Earnest, Bible-believing Christians have not always seen eye to eye on such matters, and sometimes their quarrels have been noisy and divisive.

Salvation is impossible on our own.

In this chapter, we shall review some of the classic debates about grace and look at some of the terms that are often used in this ongoing struggle. We cannot possibly resolve all of these differences in these few pages, but we will seek for better understanding. Where we must in good conscience differ from one another in interpretation of certain aspects of God's grace, let us do so with love and humility remembering the words of the great missionary statesman Luther Rice:

> Let us not, however, become bitter against those who view this matter [the doctrine of election] in a different light, nor treat them in a supercilious manner; rather let us be gentle towards all men. For who has made us to differ from what we once were? Who has removed the scales from our eyes?[4]

Augustine: The Teacher of Grace

The first great battle over the doctrine of grace in the history of the church took place more than 300 years after the death of the apostle Paul. This involved a terrific struggle between St. Augustine, one of the greatest theologians who ever lived, and Pelagius, a British monk and moral reformer who stressed the ability of human beings to make themselves pleasing to God by obeying the law. Later Christians referred to Augustine as *doctor gratiae,* "the teacher of grace," because his influence was so great in this area.

Augustine's theology of grace grew out of his own experience of utter impotence and helplessness before God. In his famous autobiography, *The Confessions,* Augustine described his struggle and failure to live a life pleasing to God:

From the mud of my fleshly desires … belched out murky clouds that obscured and darkened my heart until I could not distinguish the calm light of love from the fog of lust. The two swirled about together and dragged me … over the cliffs of my desires, and engulfed me in a whirlpool of sins. … I poured myself out, frothed and floundered in the tumultuous sea of my fornications; and you were silent. … By your sheer grace and mercy you melted my sins away like ice.[5]

In his search for peace, Augustine tried many religions and schools of thought. For several years he was a follower of Manichaeanism, a fatalistic religion based on radical dualism: light and darkness, good and evil locked forever in a great cosmic battle. Then he became a skeptic, a philosophy that denied the possibility of absolute truth. His conversion to Christ occurred as he was sitting in a garden reading a passage from Romans 13. In this moment he realized that his self-striving was useless and would never lead him to God. By God's grace he resolved to "put on the Lord Jesus Christ" (v. 14, NASB). Then immediately, he said, "the light of certainty flooded my heart and all dark shades of doubt fled away."[6]

Augustine rediscovered what Paul had proclaimed: apart from the grace of Christ we are hopelessly lost and can do nothing to save ourselves. This was the basis of Augustine's prayer, "Oh Lord, give what you command, and command whatever you will." When Pelagius heard this prayer, he was infuriated because it seemed to undercut the moral nerve of the Christian faith. If we were not able to obey God's commandments, then why had He given them in the first place? Salvation, he said, comes about by the performance of good works and the fulfillment of obligations laid down by God. We can summarize the theology of Pelagius in five propositions, each of which was strongly opposed by Augustine in the course of the Pelagian controversy.

1. Adam was created mortal; he would have died had he never sinned. This view of death is as popular today as it was

Apart from the grace of Christ we are hopelessly lost and can do nothing to save ourselves.

According to Scripture, we are born in a condition of estrangement from God.

in Pelagius' day. How often have you heard death extolled as "a normal part of life," with no intrinsic connection to our moral standing before God? However, Augustine taught that "the wages of sin is death," physical as well as spiritual (Rom. 6:23). While we cannot correlate personal illness and death with the specific sins of this or that individual, we do live in a fallen world where everything in nature, including our physical bodies, is subject to the laws of decay, corruption and death. Indeed, as the Bible teaches, the whole creation is "groaning" like a woman about to give birth to a child as it yearns for the deliverance that Christ will bring at His second coming (Rom. 8:18-25).

2. Sin is transmitted by imitation, not by propagation. For Pelagius, there was no real connection between our sins and Adam's. He set us a bad example, to be sure, but that was it. Human beings are born without sin, and they commit sins only by imitating the bad examples of others. Augustine, on the other hand, developed a robust doctrine of original sin, the idea that sin is a fundamental condition of estrangement from God. Furthermore, like a hereditary disease, it is passed down from one generation to another.

3. Grace is not opposed to nature but rather is present within nature. If Augustine taught original sin, Pelagius believed in original uprightness. We do not need to be "born again," since we were born just fine the first time! If we do sin, we can reform ourselves by strenuous moral effort. Pelagius did concede that God had given two extra "umphs" of grace after creation, one in the Old Testament, the other in the New: namely, the giving of the law and the sending of Christ. The law was the perfect rule book, and Jesus was the perfect rule keeper—nothing more. Salvation, like sin, is by imitation too. Augustine, however, realized the futility of this approach. It was like setting an ostrich egg in front of a banty hen and telling her, "Now look at this one, and try harder next time!" The human situation, Augustine claimed, was far more serious than Pelagius allowed. Only a supernatural work of God which comes to sinners from outside of themselves could make any real difference in their standing before a holy God.

4. *Perfection in this life is possible.* Pelagius did not say that sinless perfection was easy, nor did he claim to be perfect himself. But he did believe that, in addition to Jesus, there were perfect people who infallibly obeyed all of God's commands. It is the worse kind of defeatism, he thought, to tell Christians in advance that perfection was unattainable. Augustine held the contrary view: Christians can make great progress in their walk with the Lord, and they should be encouraged to do so; but sin is an ever-present reality with which we must struggle until we draw our last breath. Everyday we should offer this petition from the Lord's Prayer: "Forgive us our debts" (Matt. 6:12).

5. *Predestination is subordinate to foreknowledge.* When the Bible speaks of God's predestination of the elect, Pelagius said, it is merely speaking of His ability to see into the future and ratify in advance, so to speak, what He foreknows human beings will do by their own efforts. Augustine, again following Paul, grounds predestination in "the good pleasure of his will" (Eph. 1:5, KJV). Pelagius sees predestination as God's pretemporal acknowledgement of what human beings through their own merits will do to purchase their own salvation. This interpretation, Augustine countered, allows human beings to become their own savior or co-redeemer, in which case they have themselves and not God to thank for their salvation.

How does human free agency fit into all of this? In spite of his insistence on the sovereignty of grace, Augustine never understood himself as denying the natural freedom of the will. The term *free will* itself (*liberum arbitrium* in Latin) is not found in the Bible. The second-century theologian Tertullian, who also coined the word *Trinity,* borrowed the term for Christian usage from the ancient Stoic philosophers. Augustine also spoke frequently of the human "free will," by which he meant the ability of a man or woman to act or decide freely without being compelled or forced by some external constraint. Indeed, one of the first books he wrote as a Christian was entitled *On Free Will.* It was a defense of free

When Augustine spoke of the human "free will," he meant the ability of a man or woman to act or decide freely without being compelled or forced by some external constraint.

moral agency against Manichaean determinism, the religion of fatalism from which he himself had been delivered.

For Augustine the human will is always moved in one direction or another by the object of its love. In the garden of Eden, Adam and Eve were capable of moving either toward the love of God (*amor dei*), or away from God and toward the love of self (*amor sui*). When they chose the latter, something disastrous happened both for them and for all their human descendants. Their free will was left intact in the sense that it was still *they* who acted and loved, and *they* who were therefore morally responsible for what they did; however, their free will was so distorted by sin that it was drawn away from the love of God, the true purpose for which they had been created. Now it was pulled in its innermost desires toward the love of self. In other words, human free will was so weakened by sin and the fall that it became "curved in on itself" (*incurvatus in se*). We can illustrate Augustine's conception of human free will before the fall like this:

Human free will was weakened by sin and the fall.

(amor dei)
Love of God

Human Free Will

Love of Self
(amor sui)

Human free will was not eliminated or destroyed by the fall, but it was so thoroughly contaminated, so filled with pride and self-seeking, that it was disposed now to choose objects of desire that inevitably led it further and further away from God. This is what Paul meant, Augustine said, when he declared in Romans 3:10-12 that: "There is no one righteous, not even one; there is no one who understands, no one who seeks God. All have turned away, they have together become worthless; there is no one who does good, not even one." Augustine's view of free will after the fall looks like this:

(amor dei)
Love of God

Human Free Will

Love of Self
(amor sui)

This is why Pelagius' advice about "trying harder next time" and picking ourselves up by our own bootstraps is so flawed. Anyone who has suffered from severe drug or alcohol addiction can understand Augustine's point. It is not sufficient to say to such addicts, "Just quit drinking" or "Get off drugs!" Their will has been so misshapen by their addiction that good advice alone is not enough to change their habits. Something must happen to transform them from within. Their "want to" must be changed. Augustine believed that all human beings apart from grace were addicts—addicted to sin, pride, and self-centeredness. He knew that we were created by God for fellowship with Him, and that our hearts would always be restless until they found true rest in Him. But this kind of reorientation required the operation of divine grace. As Jesus said in John 15:5 (this was one of Augustine's favorite Bible verses): "Apart from me you can do nothing." From first to last, we are absolutely dependent upon God for our salvation.

"Apart from me you can do nothing" (John 15:5).

Augustine rendered a great service to the gospel in recovering the Pauline theology of grace. Pelagius was an earnest, well-meaning moralist, but his understanding of human nature and salvation was not merely erroneous but heretical.

When the printing press was invented in the 15th century, Augustine's writings were among the first to be published.

This was recognized at the Council of Ephesus which condemned his views in 431, one year after Augustine died. Pelagian ideas still exist today in certain forms of liberal theology, the human potential movement, and even some strands of positive-thinking such as "can do" evangelicalism, which stresses self-improvement more than salvation by grace.

The influence of Augustine was great and later theologians, Protestants and Catholics alike, frequently quoted him in support of their own views. While his understanding of grace was thoroughly biblical, not all of his views were equally sound. For example, he accepted the practice of infant baptism, which is nowhere mentioned in the Bible, and connected it to his doctrine of original sin. He also believed that the sacraments were necessary channels of God's grace. This led later theologians, such as Thomas Aquinas, to construct an elaborate sacramental theology based on merit and the performance of good works which were seen as necessary conditions for remaining in "a state of grace." In this way, Pelagianism, though officially condemned, re-entered through the backdoor. When the printing press was invented in the 15th century, Augustine's writings were among the first to be published. The Protestant reformers, especially Martin Luther, John Calvin, and Thomas Cramner, were avid readers of Augustine. They discovered in "the teacher of grace," an understanding of salvation which pointed back to the apostolic message of the Scriptures.

PERSONAL LEARNING ACTIVITY
Augustine was referred to as the "teacher of grace."
Why is his emphasis on grace so important to followers of Christ?

_____

_____

Three Debates

The doctrine of grace is like an underground spring of hot water, which is always bubbling just below the surface and occasionally bursting forth into a spectacular geyser. Augustine was a great champion of grace, and his views on the subject have influenced all subsequent thinkers. But his teaching has also been qualified and modified in many ways. Each new generation, it seems, must struggle with the issues of grace and human freedom for itself. In the next chapter, we are going to see how our understanding of divine grace relates to other teachings of the Christian faith. But we must first examine three classic debates which continue to shape the way Christians understand these issues.

1. Luther and Erasmus. Martin Luther (1483-1546) was an Augustinian monk who, amidst many struggles, came to a new understanding of God, faith, and the church based on his study of the Holy Scriptures. The heart of Luther's theology was that in Jesus Christ the sovereign God has given Himself, utterly and without reserve, for us. The gift of salvation, he said, must be appropriated by faith alone. To have faith is to accept the salvation which is ours in Jesus Christ. But saving faith is not a self-generated human activity; it is a gift of the Holy Spirit. Luther's great discovery of the gospel became the watchword of the Reformation: *Justification by grace alone, through faith alone, in Jesus Christ alone.*

The Dutch humanist, Desiderius Erasmus (1469-1536) was the greatest scholar of the 16th century, and he agreed with Luther's criticism of the abuses in the church. He also edited the first published edition of the Greek New Testament, which Luther used to develop his Reformation theology. Thus some have said, "Erasmus laid the egg that Luther hatched!" In 1524, however, Erasmus published a treatise on the freedom of the will in which he attacked Luther's strong Augustinian understanding of grace. Erasmus was not a pure Pelagian for he did recognize the necessity of grace. But he underestimated the devastating impact of the fall in tilting human beings away from God. Consequently, he failed to see

In Jesus Christ the sovereign God has given Himself, utterly and without reserve, for us.

(what even Thomas Aquinas understood) that it does not lie in the power of sinful human beings to begin the journey to salvation apart from the special intervention of God's grace.

Part of the difficulty arose from Erasmus' definition of free will as the power "by which a man can apply himself to the things which lead to eternal salvation, or turn away from them."[7] This definition confuses the natural capacity of human beings to make non-coerced choices, which Augustine and Luther gladly admit, with that true freedom from sin and death which Paul referred to as "the glorious freedom of the children of God" (Rom. 8:21). This is the kind of freedom Jesus had in mind when He said, "You shall know the truth, and the truth shall make you free" (John 8:32, NKJV). On the basis of Erasmus' definition, not even the saints in heaven would be free, for there they are not constantly confronted with the "choice" of remaining with God in bliss or joining Satan and the damned in the inferno. But who could imagine that in heaven we will be unfree, deprived somehow of free moral agency? To the contrary, heaven will be the "freest" of all places! We shall be liberated from the presence of sin as well as from its penalty and power. For all eternity we shall freely and joyfully worship God and enjoy Him forever.

God desires that we should be truly free in our love toward Him.

Luther responded to Erasmus' attack in a treatise of his own, *The Bondage of the Will,* published in 1525. In the heat of the argument, Luther used the language of "necessity," and this has led some scholars to accuse him of fatalism. But in speaking of the will's bondage, Luther was merely developing an image originally drawn by Jesus: "Everyone who sins is a slave to sin" and "You belong to your father, the devil, and you want to carry out your father's desires" (John 8:34,44). God clearly desires that we should be truly free in our love toward Him, Luther says, but this is not a possibility until we have been first *freed* from our captivity to Satan and self.

When he tried to square this teaching with the doctrine of predestination, Luther realized that he had entered the realm of mystery. There are, he suggested, three lights—the light of nature, the light of grace, and the light of glory. By the light of grace we are able to understand many problems which appeared insoluble by the light of nature, that is, apart from God's special revelation in the Bible. Even so, in the light of glory, God's righteous judgments—incomprehensible to us now even by the light of grace—will be openly manifested. Luther thus appealed to the eschatological vindication of God's plan of redemption in eternity. Ultimately, when we shall have proceeded through the "lights" of nature and grace into the light of glory, what now seems hidden and mysterious will be openly manifest for all the universe to see.

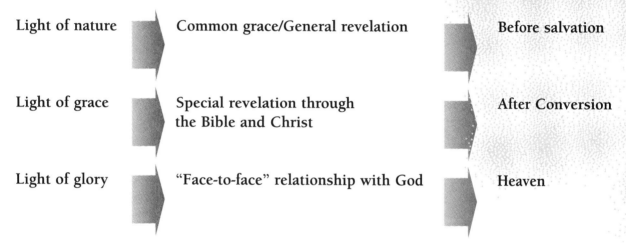

Light of nature	Common grace/General revelation	Before salvation
Light of grace	Special revelation through the Bible and Christ	After Conversion
Light of glory	"Face-to-face" relationship with God	Heaven

As a pastor, Luther was often asked to counsel with ordinary Christians who were upset about the riddles of grace and election. Typical was his response to Barbara Lisskirchen, who was distressed that she was not among the elect:

> When such thoughts assail you, you should learn to ask yourself, "If you please, in which Commandment is it written that I should think about and deal with this matter?" When it appears that there is no such Commandment, learn to say: "Begone, wretched devil! You are trying to make me worry about myself. But God declares everywhere that I should let him care for me."... The highest of all God's commands is this, that

we hold up before our eyes the image of his dear Son, our Lord Jesus Christ. Every day he should be our excellent mirror wherein we behold how much God loves us and how well, in his infinite goodness, he has cared for us in that he gave his dear Son for us. In this way, I say, and in no other, does one learn how to deal properly with the question of predestination. It will be manifest that you believe in Christ. If you believe, then you are called. And if you are called, then you are most certainly predestinated. Do not let this mirror and throne of grace be torn away from before your eyes. … contemplate … Christ given for us. Then, God willing, you will feel better.[8]

The mystery of election, Luther teaches us, can only be approached through the cross, through the "wounds of Jesus." It is not a matter for speculation and theological debate. Instead, it is a window into the gracious will of the God who spared not His own Son but freely gave Him up for us all.

2. Calvinists and Arminians. John Calvin (1509-1564) was a second-generation reformer who took many of Luther's ideas and transplanted them to the city of Geneva which became the nerve center of international Protestantism. Calvin's ideas radiated out from Switzerland to Hungary and Poland in the East, and to Scotland and the Netherlands in the West. Eventually they were brought to the New World by the Pilgrims and the Puritans. The greatest theologian of New England was a Calvinist, Jonathan Edwards.

Calvin's name is forever linked with the doctrine of predestination which he undoubtedly believed and taught in a strict Augustinian form. But he also warned against parading the message of election before novices in the faith. He urged his followers to say no more about predestination than could be derived from the Bible. Since God alone knows whom He has elected to salvation, we must preach the gospel to everyone. We must trust the Holy Spirit to use it as an effective means for calling to faith those who have been chosen in

"We should not investigate what the Lord has left hidden in secret that we should not neglect what he has brought into the open, so that we may not be convicted of excessive curiosity on the one hand, or of excessive ingratitude on the other."[9]
–John Calvin

Christ before the foundation of the world. Predestination, as Calvin understood it, is neither a church steeple from which to view the human landscape, nor a soft pillow on which to sleep. It is rather a stronghold in times of temptations and trials and a confession of praise to God's grace and to His glory.

Was Calvin himself always faithful to his own advice about not speculating beyond the bounds of revelation? Perhaps not. Later Calvinists certainly seem to have forgotten his words as they became embroiled in endless debates over the ordering of God's decrees, evidences of election in one's activity in the world, the extent of the atonement, and so forth. Theodore Beza, Calvin's successor in Geneva, and William Perkins, a Puritan theologian in England, among others, attempted to recast Calvin's biblical theology in a more systematic, logically rigorous form. For them the doctrine of predestination became the starting point for theology. This was going far beyond Calvin for whom predestination was a fact of Scripture, but not the controlling principle of all doctrine.

In early 17th-century Holland, a fierce debate arose over the doctrine of election between strict Calvinists and Arminians (so called from Jacob Arminius, a professor at Leyden University), who sought a looser formulation of Reformation theology. Soon the whole Dutch nation became embroiled in this dispute. Predestination was the topic of discussion in the marketplace as well as in the pulpit. Common people argued about election and the mysteries of grace in towboats and in taverns, from the fish market to the courthouse. The conflict was exacerbated by political and social factors. From 1618 to 1619, an international assembly of Reformation theologians gathered at the Synod of Dort to resolve the controversy. In response to certain theses put forth by the Arminians (also called the Remonstrants), the Synod of Dort outlined the orthodox Calvinist understanding of salvation in terms of five central principles, often called "the five points of Calvinism." Because tulips are the national flower of Holland where the city of Dort is located, these ideas are sometimes arranged in the form of the following acrostic:

Predestination, as Calvin understood it, is a stronghold in times of temptations and trials and a confession of praise to God's grace and to His glory.

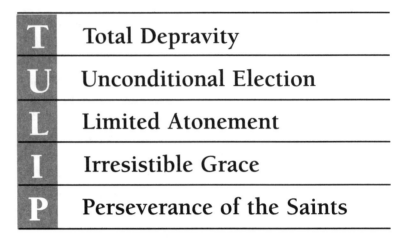

T	Total Depravity
U	Unconditional Election
L	Limited Atonement
I	Irresistible Grace
P	Perseverance of the Saints

Arminius held strongly to the Protestant teaching of justification by faith alone.

It is important to point out that this was an intra-Reformed argument. In fact, Arminius himself was much closer in many of his ideas to Calvin than to some latter-day Arminians. Arminius was certainly no Pelagian. Far more than Erasmus, he realized that human free will had been seriously damaged by the fall. He also believed that only as human beings were endowed with faith through the Holy Spirit could they really love God and exercise the freedom from which they were created. For Arminius, however, grace was resistible and the atonement was universal in its scope. Predestination was based on God's foreknowledge, but not (as Pelagius had supposed) on His foreknowledge of foreseen merits. It was rather God's foreknowledge of foreseen *faith,* which conditioned His election of believers. In this way, Arminius held strongly to the Protestant teaching of justification by faith alone while at the same time qualifying the Augustinian-Calvinist doctrine of predestination in a significant way. In the next chapter, we shall revisit the so-called "five points of Calvinism." It is important to note that both evangelical Calvinists and evangelical Arminians affirm the reality of God's grace, although they differ among themselves on its implications for other doctrines.

3. Wesley and Whitefield. Between the death of Arminius in 1609 and the birth of John Wesley in 1703,

Arminianism as a system of thought lost much of its evangelical emphasis. Many Arminians became rationalists or deists denying biblical miracles and the supernatural origins of the Christian faith. Others were drawn into Unitarianism repudiating both the doctrine of the Trinity and the divinity of Christ. However, not all Arminians followed this path. The Great Awakening of the 18th century was led by two anointed servants of God: one a Calvinist, George Whitefield; the other an Arminian, John Wesley.

Whitefield and Wesley were good friends from their student days at Oxford when both were members of the "Holy Club," a nickname given to those who followed a disciplined life of study and prayer. Both men were "savingly converted" in the 1730s and became leaders in the great revival that was sweeping through England. Whitefield made 13 trips across the Atlantic bringing the fires of awakening to the American colonies, while Wesley traveled by horseback some 225,000 miles organizing Methodist societies throughout Britain.

Wesley and Whitefield held differing views about the doctrine of predestination which led to a strain on their friendship. Wesley once admitted that he was just "a hair's breadth" from Calvinism. He believed strongly in the sovereignty of God, the doctrine of original sin, and the necessity of the new birth, but could not accept the ideas of unconditional election and irresistible grace. Neither did he believe in the perseverance of the saints. Salvation once received could be forfeited, he thought, by falling into serious sin. On all of these issues, Whitefield remained a Calvinist. He also refused to accept Wesley's ideas about sinless perfection.

After many years of disagreement and disputation, both men realized their differences would not likely be settled this side of heaven. Through the influence of mutual friends, including Charles Wesley, John's hymn-writing brother, the two great evangelists were reconciled. The theological differences remained—and there was no effort to sweep them under the rug—but their love for the lost and their common commitment to the gospel far outweighed their disputes.

John Wesley traveled by horseback some 225,000 miles organizing Methodist societies throughout Britain.

Whitefield died on September 30, 1770, in Newburyport, Massachusetts. He had requested that his memorial service in England be conducted by his old friend, John Wesley. On this occasion Wesley spoke movingly of Whitefield's many labors for the Lord, his tenderheartedness, his charitable spirit, his loyalty and friendship. He concluded with a question, "Have we read or heard of any person, who called so many thousands, so many myriads of sinners to repentance?"[10]

The love and mutual respect Whitefield and Wesley had for each other, despite their strong doctrinal divergence, was an important example for later generations of Christians. During both the First and Second Great Awakenings in America, Baptists, Methodists, Presbyterians, and other evangelical Christians worked together sharing the good news of salvation through Jesus Christ alone. Wesley and Whitefield demonstrated that Bible-believing Christians can disagree in love and still stand together as partners in sharing Jesus' love with the lost. Evangelical unity based on the gospel became a guiding principle in the ministry of other leaders including Charles Haddon Spurgeon, D.L. Moody, and Billy Graham.

Wesley and Whitefield collaborated in the formation of Bible societies, missionary enterprises, as well as works of charity and benevolence.

PERSONAL LEARNING ACTIVITY
Wesley and Whitefield demonstrated that Christians can disagree and still be partners in the sharing of Jesus' love. What can you learn from their example that would impact your service to Christ in your church?

_____

As you relate to others at home, school, work, and in recreation?

_____

Principles of Unity

Perhaps you wonder how Christians who hold different views about the nature of predestination, or the extent of the atonement, or the ordering of God's decrees can remain in fellowship with one another much less work together in a common evangelistic effort. First, let me suggest three paths we must *not* take in our quest for a harmonius result.

1. We do not achieve unity by compromising our convictions. In discussing matters about which Christians differed with one another, Paul said, "Each one should be fully convinced in his own mind. ... Why do you judge your brother? Or why do you look down on your brother? For we will all stand before God's judgment seat" (Rom. 14:5,10).

2. We must never seek togetherness for mere prudential reasons. In the same chapter in which Jesus prayed that His disciples might be one, He also asked the Father to sanctify them in the truth (see John 17:17,21). God's inerrant Word is the infallible standard to which we must always appeal in our efforts to understand the things of God more fully.

3. We must never imagine that doctrinal matters are trivial or unimportant. In some circles this slogan is popular: "Missions unites but doctrine divides." This statement has an alluring appeal, but it is basically false for there is no such thing as missions apart from doctrine. We have no message, no gospel apart from "the faith that was once for all entrusted to the saints" (Jude 3). A church with no doctrinal moorings or with shaky theological foundations will soon be a church with nothing to say to a lost and dying world.

Thinking constructively, how can we work together in a common Christian cause without violating these principles? Consider these suggestions:

• *Make a careful distinction between primary doctrines of the faith which may not be compromised without betraying the gospel, and secondary issues which may be important but are not essential for fellowship.* Everything in God's Word is true and important or else it would not be there, but not everything is of equal importance in every respect. Thus Paul, in describing the

There is no such thing as missions apart from doctrine.

Christians can have honest disagreements about the interpretation of certain doctrines and still worship and work together.

heart of the gospel, spoke of those matters that are "of first importance" (1 Cor. 15:3). The second coming of Christ, for example, is a cardinal doctrine of the Christian faith. To deny it is to lapse into serious heresy. But earnest, Bible-believing Christians may honestly differ on some details of the end times. Local churches and various associations of Christians set forth their distinctive beliefs in confessions of faith. These documents are not infallible, but they do identify a consensual interpretation of the Bible within a given community of faith. For this reason, they are very useful in helping Christians to distinguish primary and secondary matters of faith. We must never forget, of course, that all such confessions are accountable to, and revisable in light of, the Bible.

• *When we have theological disagreements with our brothers and sisters in Christ, it is always appropriate for us to pray for additional guidance and illumination from the Holy Spirit.* John Robinson, the pastor of the Pilgrim Fathers, once said to his flock: "The Lord had more truth and light yet to break forth out of his holy word."[11] The same Spirit who inspired the Scriptures long ago must be present in our hearts and minds when we study them today if we are to understand them.

• *Humility, not arrogance, is the proper attitude in all controversies among Christians.* This is not an argument for proceeding from lack of conviction, but for recognizing our own limitations and blind spots. The wisest among us are still learners in the school of faith.

PERSONAL LEARNING ACTIVITY
Review the three principles for working with other Christians without compromising our convictions. Which one is most important? Why?

_____

_____

Returning from these general principles to the doctrine of grace which we have surveyed historically throughout this chapter, we may take a parting notice of John Wesley by listening in on a conversation he had with Charles Simeon on December 20, 1784. At this point in his life, Wesley was already an old man. Whitefield had been dead for 14 years, while Wesley would live seven more. Simeon, like Wesley and Whitefield, was a leader of the evangelical revival in Great Britain. He agreed more with Whitefield than Wesley on the doctrines of grace, but he recognized that Wesley was a great servant of the Lord. He sought to establish a common basis with him on those theological principles which mattered most to both of them. This is Simeon's account of his conversation with Wesley:

Christians are agreed that there is no hope for salvation apart from the grace of God.

Simeon: "Sir, I understand that you are called an Arminian; and I have been sometimes called a Calvinist; and therefore I suppose we are to draw daggers. But before I consent to begin the combat, with your permission I will ask you a few questions. ... Pray, Sir, do you feel yourself a depraved creature, so depraved that you would never have thought of turning to God, if God had not first put it into your heart?"

Wesley: "Yes, I do indeed."

Simeon: "And do you utterly despair of recommending yourself to God by anything you can do; and look for salvation solely through the blood and righteousness of Christ?"

Wesley: "Yes, solely through Christ."

Simeon: "But, Sir, supposing you were at first saved by Christ, are you not somehow or other to save yourself afterwards by your own works?"

Wesley: "No, I must be saved by Christ from first to last."

Simeon: "Allowing, then, that you were first turned by the grace of God, are you not in some way or other to keep yourself by your own power?"

As Christians, we can unite around the great truths of the gospel and our task to proclaim this message to all people.

Wesley: "No."

Simeon: "What, then, are you to be upheld every hour and every moment by God, as much as an infant in its mother's arms?"

Wesley: "Yes, altogether."

Simeon: "And is all your hope in the grace and mercy of God to preserve you unto His heavenly kingdom?"

Wesley: "Yes, I have no hope but in Him."

Simeon: "Then, Sir, with your leave I will put up my dagger again; for this is all my Calvinism; this is my election, my justification by faith, my final perseverance: it is in substance all that I hold, and as I hold it; and therefore, if you please, instead of searching out terms and phrases to be a ground of contention between us, we will cordially unite in those things wherein we agree."[12]

---

[1] J. I. Packer, *Evangelism and the Sovereignty of God* (London: Inter-Varsity Press, 1961), 17.

[2] Ella Wheeler Wilcox, "Will," in *Maurine and Other Poems* (Chicago: W. B. Conkey Company, 1888), 144.

[3] William Ernest Henley, "Invictus," in *The Best Loved Poems of the American People,* Hazel Felleman, ed., (New York: Garden City Publishing Co., 1936), 73.

[4] James B. Taylor, *Memoir of Rev. Luther Rice* (Baltimore: Armstrong and Berry, 1841), 293-94.

[5] St. Augustine, *The Confessions,* Maria Boulding, trans., John E. Rotelle, ed., 2.2, 2.4, (New York: New City Press, 1997), 62-63, 72.

[6] Ibid., 8.29, 207.

[7] E. Gordon Rupp and Philip S. Watson, eds., *The Library of Christian Classics—Luther and Erasmus: Free Will and Salvation,* vol. XVII, (Philadelphia: The Westminster Press, 1969), 47.

[8] Theodore G. Tappert, ed., *The Library of Christian Classics—Luther: Letters of Spiritual Counsel,* vol. XVIII, (Philadelphia: The Westminster Press, 1955), 116.

[9] John T. McNeill, ed., and Ford Lewis Battles, trans., *The Library of Christian Classics—Calvin: Institutes of the Christian Religion,* vol. XXI, (Philadelphia: The Westminster Press, 1960), 925.

[10] From *George Whitefield* by Arnold A. Dallimore, copyright © 1990, page 197. Used by permission of Crossway Books, a division of Good News Publishers, Wheaton, Illinois 60187.

[11] Timothy George, *John Robinson and the English Separatist Tradition* (Macon, GA: Mercer University Press, 1982), 91.

[12] Packer, *Evangelism,* 14.

A Graceful Theology

CHAPTER FOUR

When you go shopping at the grocery store, do you take time to read the labels on the food you are about to buy? I do. Labels often have important information about the product within—its ingredients, fiber content, fat grams, how many calories per serving, and so forth. More recently, though, I became skeptical about such labels for I have discovered that they sometimes distort as much as they reveal. Food labels and claims can be very confusing. Becoming a wise shopper means learning how to decipher the labels. There may be hidden ingredients not listed at all, or cancer-causing preservatives not identified as such. Labels can be libels. They can be downright dangerous!

This is also true in human relationships. *Communist, redneck, egghead, liberal, fundamentalist*—all these terms carry negative baggage. They are frequently used in a pejorative manner to dismiss someone we do not like without taking him or her seriously as a person. *Calvinist* and *Arminian,* while historically justifiable when properly defined, can also become labels with which fellow Christians attack and reproach one another. Thus, "He's a Calvinist!" might mean that he is a mean-spirited, pigheaded, hard-nosed bully who never has any fun and doesn't want anybody else to! Conversely, "She's an Arminian!" might mean she's a weak-kneed, lily-livered, mushy-minded pushover who has no convictions and won't stand up for what's right! If possible, it would be best to eliminate both terms from our vocabulary. However, since this is not a realistic option, at least we ought to be careful and cautious in our use of them. In all relationships, we do well to remember Paul's word of counsel: "Let us therefore make every effort to do what leads to peace and to mutual edification" (Rom. 14:19).

To clarify matters, we shall do three things in this chapter.

The devil again succeeds in laying his cuckoo eggs in a pious nest. ... The sulphurous stench of hell is as nothing compared to the evil odor emitted by divine grace gone putrid.[1]
–Helmut Thielicke

First, we shall consider the question, "Are Baptists Calvinists?" Next, we shall look briefly at the so-called five points of Calvinism which have traditionally been called "the doctrines of grace." And, finally, we shall look at several serious pitfalls to avoid as we seek to understand the Bible's teaching concerning "the manifold grace of God" (1 Pet. 4:10, NKJV).

Are Baptists Calvinists?

Christians of all denominations have wrestled with the mystery of God's sovereignty and human freedom. The Baptist movement as we know it today began in early 17th-century England. Those called Baptists shared many things in common including a strong commitment to biblical authority, salvation by grace through faith in Christ alone, believer's baptism by immersion, and religious liberty. However, by 1650, there were two distinct streams of Baptist life in England: one inclined to Calvinistic views on election (called Particular Baptists because they believed that Christ had died for particular persons); the other more in line with Arminian views on this subject (called General Baptists for their belief that the atonement was general or universal in scope). By the 18th century, both groups had suffered from extremist tendencies. Many of the Generals lost their evangelical beliefs and drifted into Unitarianism, while most of the Particulars so emphasized God's sovereignty that they neglected evangelism. As a result of a revival led by Whitefield and Wesley, both groups experienced an evangelical resurgence, and later in the 19th century these two streams united forming the Baptist Union of Great Britain. Charles Haddon Spurgeon, perhaps the greatest preacher Baptists have ever known, combined a staunch Calvinistic theology with strong, evangelistic ministry.

Baptists in America debated the same issues. But the influence of the Philadelphia *Baptist Confession* (first printed by Benjamin Franklin in 1742) and the writings of Baptist theologian Andrew Fuller reinforced the evangelical Calvinism of most mainstream Baptists. In the first decade of the 19th century, David Benedict, a Baptist historian from Rhode

> Throughout history Christians of all denominations have wrestled with the mystery of God's sovereignty and human freedom.

Island, made an extensive tour of Baptist churches throughout America. He gave the following summary of the Baptist theology he encountered:

> Take this denomination at large, I believe the following will be found a pretty correct statement of their views of doctrine. They hold that man in his natural condition is entirely depraved and sinful; that unless he is born again—changed by grace—or made alive unto God—he cannot be fitted for the communion of saints on earth, nor the enjoyment of God in Heaven; that where God hath begun a good work, he will carry it on to the end; that there is an election of grace—an effectual calling, etc. and that the happiness of the right-eous and the misery of the wicked will both be eternal.[2]

With some notable exceptions such views were typical of Baptists, northern and southern, until the Civil War, and for several decades following. Baptists strongly rejected the anti-missionary, anti-evangelistic ideas of hyper-Calvinism while they affirmed both human responsibility and the mystery of God's sovereignty in salvation. As late as 1905, F. H. Kerfoot, a systematic theologian in Louisville, said, "Nearly all Baptists believe what are usually termed the 'doctrines of grace.'"[3] His successor, E.Y. Mullins, disliked the labels *Calvinist* and *Arminian* and sought to transcend the controversy altogether. While retaining much of the content of traditional Reformed theology, he gave it a new casting by restating it in terms of his distinctive theology of experience. Mullins' counterpart in the North, Augustus H. Strong, attempted to harmonize Calvinistic theology with modern science and philosophy. At Southwestern Seminary in Texas, W.T. Conner, who studied with both Mullins and Strong, extended their views seeking to balance a theology of grace with the call to evangelism and missions. One notable exception to this pattern was Dale Moody who promoted an unabridged Arminianism, even calling into question the eternal security of the believer.

Baptists strongly rejected the anti-missionary, anti-evangelistic ideas of hyper-Calvinism while they affirmed both human responsibility and the mystery of God's sovereignty in salvation.

Southern Baptists are people who believe the Bible, the Word of God, is their final written authority.

Are Baptists Calvinists? This question does not admit of a simple yes-or-no answer for, as we have seen, Baptists historically have been all over the map on the Calvinist-Arminian divide. What can be said without dispute, however, is that there is a strong Calvinist or Reformed stream within the Baptist tradition and that this perspective has been held by some of the most notable shapers of Baptist life and thought. Baptists may not agree on how to resolve (the perhaps unresolvable) tension between divine sovereignty and human free agency, but all Bible-believing Baptists will affirm what the Bible clearly teaches—first, God is sovereign and no one is ever saved by anything they do, but only and totally by an act of God; second, human beings are not robots but are fully responsible to God for their actions. They have a duty to repent and believe the gospel. And Christians also have a duty to share the good news of Jesus with everyone everywhere.

Some critics seem to take a perverse delight when Christians committed to the authority of the Bible are unable to see eye to eye. Nothing pleases the devil more than when evangelical believers aim their arrows at one another rather than at him! But God's grace should be a cause for celebration, not division. It is a mark of humility to say: "I may be mistaken about this or that detail concerning the decrees of God or the mystery of election. Let's search the Scriptures together." Dr. Paige Patterson, recent president of the Southern Baptist Convention, has spoken wisely on this matter:

> [He] described Southern Baptists as a people who believe the Bible to be the Word of God as their final authority, that salvation is by grace through faith alone and that adult-like faith witnessed by believer's baptism provides a testimony to a watching world. If we believe those things all fall within the purview of the Baptist faith, then there's plenty of room for all of us in these various emphases that we bring. There's plenty of room under the umbrella for anyone who is anything from a one- to five-point Calvinist.[4]

PERSONAL LEARNING ACTIVITY
How would you answer the question:
Are Baptists Calvinists?

_____

_____

There is room under the umbrella for believers who hold different positions, as it relates to Calvinism.

From Tulips to Roses

Some differences among Christians are substantial and real, while others stem from misunderstandings and miscommunications. To some extent, perhaps, the latter is the case with the so-called five points of Calvinism. As we saw in chapter 3, these theological terms do not come directly from John Calvin, but rather from a post-Reformation controversy in Holland. When we lift that historical debate out of context and bring it into our own discussions, the result can be misleading and artificial. It would be better if we could stop talking about "points" at all! In a certain sense, there is only one point—the God of grace and glory. In another sense, there are at least 66 points, since every book in the Bible sets forth the gospel of grace. However, the doctrines of grace are often presented in terms of these theological ideas, and we should understand what is meant by them.

To clarify these terms, I suggest a different acrostic. Instead of the traditional TULIP, I recommend that we think of ROSES. Instead of total depravity, let's think about radical depravity. Rather than unconditional election, let's posit sovereign election. In the place of limited atonement, let's put singular (or particular) redemption. Finally, irresistible grace becomes overcoming grace, and perseverance of the saints becomes eternal life.

R	Radical Depravity
O	Overcoming Grace
S	Sovereign Election
E	Eternal Life
S	Singular Redemption

We are born as rebels inheriting a corrupted nature from our parents and growing up in an environment tainted by sin.

Let's look briefly at each one of these:

1. Radical Depravity: From Genesis to Revelation, the Bible teaches that human beings are in a mess. We are born rebels inheriting a corrupted nature from our parents and growing up in an environment tainted by sin. The Bible describes sin in many ways: missing the mark, taking the wrong path, disobeying God's law, being ruled by pride and self-interest. Sin is a universal deformity of human nature and it places men and women everywhere under the certain reign of death and the inescapable wrath of God (see Rom. 3:9-20; Eph. 2:1-3).

But *total depravity* is not the best way to express this doctrinal truth for it suggests that there is no good whatsoever in human beings, that we are always as wicked as we might possibly be. Yet this is not true. The image of God in fallen human beings has been horribly defaced by sin, but it has not been completely destroyed. *Radical depravity* is a better way of saying that we stand justly condemned before the bar of God's righteous judgment and that we can do nothing to save ourselves.

If previous generations sometimes depicted human nature in gloomy, overly pessimistic terms, the trend today is to make light of sin and its devastating effects. Cornelius Plantinga, Jr. wisely warns us against this:

For the Christian church (even in its recently popular seeker services) to ignore, euphemize, or otherwise mute the lethal reality of sin is to cut the nerve of the gospel. For the sober truth is that without full disclosure on sin, the gospel of grace becomes impertinent, unnecessary, and finally uninteresting.[5]

In other words, when we belittle sin, we minimize grace. And the contrary is also true; only when we realize the enormity of our sin can we appreciate the inexhaustible abundance of God's mercy and love. As Paul put it in Romans 5:20: "Where sin increased, grace increased all the more."

The real question raised by the doctrine of radical depravity is how pathetic fallen human beings are apart from grace. Are they merely sick, morally weak, or are they spiritually dead? The Bible says the latter in Ephesians 2:1-2: "As for you, you were dead in your transgressions and sins, in which you used to live when you followed the ways of this world." Obviously, Paul was talking to people who were physically alive and active—they ate, slept, walked, and so forth—but they were so estranged from God that their very lives were marked by death. This is why the Bible describes becoming a Christian as a resurrection, a rising to new life. This spiritual reality is vividly portrayed in Christian baptism: "We were therefore buried with him through baptism into death in order that, just as Christ was raised from the dead through the glory of the Father, we too may live a new life" (Rom. 6:4).

It is only when we realize the enormity of our sin that we can appreciate the inexhaustible abundance of God's mercy and love.

PERSONAL LEARNING ACTIVITY
What is the difference between radical depravity and total depravity?

_____

_____

2. Overcoming Grace: The term *irresistible grace* is misleading because it seems to suggest that sinners are drawn to God in a mechanical, impersonal way, as a piece of metal is to a magnet. When pressed very far, this image eliminates human free agency and moral responsibility altogether. In the Bible, not only *can* grace be resisted—it invariably *is:* Jonah runs away from God; David sins and tries to cover up his transgression; Peter denies Jesus; and so forth. Like wayward sheep, we have all resisted and gone astray (see Isa. 53:6). I like the term *overcoming grace* because it conveys the truth witnessed by so many Christians: Despite their stubbornness and rebellion, they say, God did not give up on them. Like a persistent lover, He kept on wooing until, at last, His very persistence won the day. His love and mercy overcame their rebellious resistance. And thus they confess:

> I sought the Lord, and afterward I knew he moved
> my soul to seek him, seeking me; it was not I that found,
> O Savior true; no, I was found, was found of thee.[6]

Another term for *overcoming grace* is *effectual calling*. It means simply that God is able to accomplish what He has determined to do in the salvation of lost men and women. Arminians are right to protest the notions of mechanical necessity and impersonal determinism suggested (and sadly sometimes taught) under the banner of *irresistible grace*. God created human beings with free moral agency, and He does not violate this even in the supernatural work of regeneration. Christ does not rudely bludgeon His way into the human heart. He does not abrogate our creaturely freedom. No, He beckons and woos, He pleads and pursues, He waits and wins. As Charles Spurgeon put it in one of his sermons: "With hands loaded with love he stands outside the door of your heart. Is not this good reason for opening the door and letting the heavenly stranger in, when he can bless you to such a vast extent of benediction?"[7] (see Rev. 3:20).

God is able to accomplish what He has determined to do in the salvation of lost men and women.

74

PERSONAL LEARNING ACTIVITY

Why does the author say that overcoming grace is a better term than irresistible grace?

_____

_____

3. Sovereign Election: What is election? According to the *Baptist Source Book,* election is "the gracious purpose of God, according to which He regenerates, sanctifies, and glorifies sinners. … It is a glorious display of God's sovereign goodness, and is infinitely wise, holy, and unchangeable. It excludes boasting and promotes humility."[8] Election is unconditional in the sense that it is not based upon our decision for God, but rather God's decision for us. This is what Paul means in Romans 9:16: "It does not, therefore, depend on man's desire or effort, but on God's mercy." But the adjective *unconditional* can be misleading for describing election, if it suggests (as some have taken it to mean) that God's election to salvation does not involve a genuine human response or, even worse, that God elects some people irrespective of Jesus' atoning death on the cross. J.I. Packer defines the biblical doctrine of election in this way:

> Before Creation God selected out of the human race, foreseen as fallen, those whom he would redeem, bring to faith, justify, and glorify in and through Jesus Christ (Rom. 8:28-39; Eph. 1:3-14; 2 Thess. 2:13-14; 2 Tim. 1:9-10). This divine choice is an expression of free and sovereign grace, for it is unconstrained and unconditional, not merited by anything in those who are its subjects. God owes sinners no mercy of any kind, only condemnation; so it is a wonder, and matter for endless praise, that he should choose to save any of us;

Election is not based on human desire and effort, but on God's mercy.

and doubly so when his choice involved the giving of his own Son to suffer as sin-bearer for the elect (Rom. 8:32)."[9]

The phrase "foreseen as fallen" in this definition refers to a technical debate in Reformed theology concerning the ordering of God's decrees. Those who hold, as Packer does, that God's decision to predestine some to election presupposes the fall of humanity, are known as *infralapsarians*. The alternative view, known as *supralapsariansism,* regards election as prior to the fall. No one should be overly dogmatic about such distinctions for at best we can only draw inferences from the Scriptures on this matter. We should note, however, that the *infralapsarian* view allows for a stronger declaration of human responsibility and thus is more in keeping with the thrust of the entire biblical message.

What about double predestination? Does God elect some for salvation and others for damnation in the same way? Some teachers in the Christian tradition have thought so. The ninth-century monk Gottschalk of Orbais developed a doctrine of "twin predestination" (*gemina praedestinatio*)—the belief that election and reprobation are symmetrical or side by side in God's will. This view has also been taught by some Calvinist theologians as well. But when the Bible speaks of the reprobate (as it does in Rom. 9:14-24 and 1 Pet. 2:8), it depicts their "hardening" and eventual damnation as the result of their own disobedience and rebellion against God. God passes them by, and gives them over to the sinful desires of their own hearts (see Rom. 1:24-32). The doctrine of double predestination, as sometimes presented by overly zealous Calvinists, has led many people astray. In one of the Bible's most graphic descriptions of eternal separation from God, Paul reminded the Thessalonians that "God is just" (2 Thess. 1:6). No lost sinner who ever comes before the judgment bar of God will be able to blame his eternal condemnation on the fact that he was not elected. The grace of God that brings salvation has appeared to all persons, and each will be held

> **No lost sinner who ever comes before the judgment bar of God will be able to blame his eternal condemnation on the fact that he was not elected.**

responsible for the light he or she has received (see Titus 2:11). Moreover, as Ray Summers once observed, the fact that God elects some to salvation is not an indication of injustice where others are concerned; it is an indication of grace where anyone is concerned.

In the meantime, no Christian should attempt to identify the reprobate by name, to pick them out of the crowd. The thief on the cross got in just under the wire and so have many others, though no one is promised a last-minute conversion and to presume on the grace of God is utter folly. In the final analysis, however, God is the only census taker of heaven. He alone knows the number of the elect. The Good Shepherd alone knows the identity of the sheep who belong to Him. He alone calls each one of them by name (see John 10:1-10). The Heavenly Father alone knows His adopted children, all those whom He has chosen, called, justified, and one day will glorify through His Son Jesus Christ (see Rom. 8:29-30). Thus we should view every person we meet as potentially numbered among the elect, knowing that anyone who repents and turns to Christ in faith will be saved. This conviction should lead us to share the truth of the gospel with every person who crosses our paths. C.H. Spurgeon once complained that some of his fellow Calvinists seemed to be "half afraid that perhaps some may overstep the bounds of election and get saved who should not be"! He then gave the following illustration to show the generosity of a truly graceful theology:

The Good Shepherd knows the sheep that belong to Him.

> A mouse had lived in a box all its life, and one day crawled up to the edge of it, and looked around on what it could see. Now the box only stood in a lumber room, but the mouse was surprised at its vastness, and exclaimed: "How big the world is!" If some bigots would get out of their box, and only look a little way round them, they would find the realm of grace to be far wider than they dream. ... There will be more in heaven than we expect to see there by a long way.[10]

PERSONAL LEARNING ACTIVITY
The author suggests that God is the only census taker of heaven. What does this mean in relation to the term *sovereign election*?

_____

_____

We are saved, and kept, by the grace of God.

4. Eternal Life: The perseverance of the saints (also called *eternal security* or referred to as "once saved, always saved") is the one point of Calvinism most contemporary Baptists believe without reservation. Yet these terms can all be misleading for various reasons. To persevere means to persist, to continue, to be steadfast and unrelenting in purpose. When applied to salvation doesn't this imply that, while we are saved by grace, we are kept by our own strenuous efforts? The Bible, however, attributes the fact that believers continue to abide in Christ to the keeping power of God. As Eugene Peterson translates Philippians 1:6: "There has never been the slightest doubt in my mind that the God who started this great work in you would keep at it and bring it to a flourishing finish on the very day Christ Jesus appears" (*The Message*). Nothing could be clearer: Salvation is God's work from start to finish!

Similarly, the "once saved, always saved" slogan can be misused when it is taken to mean that one can receive Jesus as Savior without also knowing Him as Lord. External religious acts such as making a profession of faith or being baptized make no one a Christian. The gospel of "easy believism" is a distortion of the biblical doctrine of perseverance. Of course, true believers can backslide and fall into heinous sin. They sometimes do. When this happens, however, they are plunged into misery for they are acting contrary to the new nature which has been imparted to them by the Holy Spirit. The Bible says the Holy Spirit is grieved, deeply offended, by sin in the life of a believer (see Eph. 4:29-32). Anyone who can sin blithely, flagrantly, flippantly with no sense of uneasiness, no qualms of conscience, is most likely a person who has never been genuinely born again in the first place. One of the marks of being a true Christian is the experience of receiving the loving discipline and chastening from the Heavenly Father (see Heb. 12:4-11).

Eternal life is not only life that lasts eternally; it is the very life of God! It can never be extinguished any more than God Himself can commit suicide. Jesus, the Good Shepherd, has given His word that those whom the Father has given Him will never perish. Instead they will be preserved to glory through all the toils and snares of their earthly journey (see John 10:28-29). Jesus Himself is the guarantee of our salvation.

Eternal life is not only life that lasts eternally; it is the very life of God!

Arminians believe that it is possible for those who have been truly born again to forfeit their salvation through radical disobedience and apostasy. They cite passages such as Hebrews 6:1-6 which can be read to support their view. On closer examination, however, this and other warning passages in the Bible are better applied to those who make a false profession of faith without being truly regenerated. Evidently Peter had this possibility in mind when he encouraged his readers "to make your calling and election sure. For if you do these things, you will never fall, and you will receive a rich welcome into the eternal kingdom of our Lord and Savior Jesus Christ" (2 Pet. 1:10-11).

Arminians have another objection to this doctrine too: they think it implies the negation of human free will. If we can resist and reject the call of Christ before conversion, then why not afterwards? Are we less free after salvation than before? If God so keeps us that we can neither utterly nor finally fall away from His grace, doesn't this mean that He violates our human freedom? The difficulty here is twofold. The first is the error Erasmus made in his debate with Luther where he confused the natural freedom of the will (better called *free moral agency*) with freedom from the penalty and power of sin.

The latter can come about only through the new birth, whereas the former is part of what it means to be a human being regardless of one's spiritual condition. Secondly, there is the failure to see that both election and perseverance "comprehends all the means in connection with the end."[11] It is we who repent, we who believe, and we who persevere to the end, although we cannot do any of this on our own. We have our gracious God alone to thank for it all from first to last.

PERSONAL LEARNING ACTIVITY

Do you agree or disagree with the statements below? Check one of the boxes for each question.

1. **Salvation is God's work from "start to finish."**
   ❏ Agree   ❏ Disagree

2. **"Easy believism" is not a distortion of the biblical doctrine of perseverance.**
   ❏ Agree   ❏ Disagree

3. **Christians are granted eternal life. It is the very life of God and it cannot be extinguished.**
   ❏ Agree   ❏ Disagree

4. **One who has been truly born again cannot forfeit his salvation through disobedience and apostasy.**
   ❏ Agree   ❏ Disagree

Christ's death is sufficient to save everyone who will live in the entire history of the world.

5. Singular Redemption: Of the five points of Calvinism, this is the one that is most controversial and also the one that is least prominent in the Scriptures. As we have seen already, *limited atonement* is a most misleading term because it suggests that there is some deficiency, something missing or lacking, in Christ's work on the cross. But Christ's death is of infinite value. It is fully sufficient to save everyone who ever lived in the entire history of the world, and, we may be so bold to declare, any other worlds inhabited by lost souls that astronomers may discover in the future. Since the Middle Ages, many theologians, including Thomas Aquinas and John Calvin, have made this distinction: Jesus' death is *sufficient* to save all, but it is *efficient* to save only those who repent and believe the gospel. Thus the Reformed position is better described as *definite atonement* or *singular redemption*— singular in the sense of having to do with specific individuals, not just with a general class or group of people. Charles Wesley, whose Arminianism was more moderate than that of his brother John, wrote a beautiful hymn describing the meaning of particular redemption in this sense:

Jesus paid for the sins of the entire human race.

> And can it be that I should gain An int'rest in the Savior's
> blood? Died He for me, who caused His pain? For me,
> who Him to death pursued? Amazing love! How can it be
> That thou my God, should die for me?[12]

The issue of the extent of the atonement is more urgent for those who believe in the penal, substitutionary atonement of Christ. The question then becomes: Did Jesus pay for the sins of the entire human race or only for those whom He knew the Father would give Him to be His own people? Those who believe in particular redemption find support for their view in verses such as Acts 20:28 where Paul spoke of "the church of God, which he bought with his own blood," and Ephesians 5:25 where we are told that "Christ loved the church and gave himself up for her." Again, in Romans 8:33-34, Paul seemed to connect election and Christ's intercession as part of a unified nexus of redemption: "Who will bring any charge against those whom God has chosen? It is God who justifies. Who is he that condemns? Christ Jesus, who died—more than that, who was raised to life—is at the right hand of God and is also interceding for us." Again in John 17:9, Jesus states that He is "not praying for the world, but for those you [the Father] have given me," and for others who would believe on Him through their witness. Clearly Jesus did not pray for everyone.

We have our gracious God alone to thank for salvation from first to last.

Did Jesus then die for those for whom He deliberately refused to pray? Further, if He fully paid for the sins of all those who perish eternally, then why are they punished? Would God be just to require them to suffer forever in hell when Jesus has already experienced hell for them, canceling their sin debt on the cross?

These are difficult questions, but those who believe in general redemption or unlimited atonement can cite numerous Scripture passages of their own which declare that Christ did die for the whole *world.* The message of John the Baptist echoes throughout the New Testament: "Behold! The Lamb of God who takes away the sin of the world!" (John 1:29, NKJV; see also 2 Cor. 5:19; 1 John 2:2; 1 Tim. 2:6; Heb. 2:9). Moreover, Peter speaks of false teachers and heretics "denying the sovereign Lord who bought them—bringing swift destruction upon themselves" (2 Pet. 2:1). These and other texts seem to indicate that *in some sense* the death of Christ is applicable to all persons without exception, including even those who will ultimately be numbered among the reprobate. The standard Calvinist response to the "all" verses is to say that they refer to all sorts or kinds of people: to princes as well as paupers, to city dwellers as well as country folk, to Africans no less than Asians, and so forth. But this is a strained exegesis which is hard to justify in every case. Unless the context clearly requires a different interpretation, it is better to say that "all means all," even if we cannot square the universal reach of Christ's atoning death with its singular focus.

However one resolves these theological and exegetical difficulties, we should not make one's views on the extent of the atonement a test of doctrinal orthodoxy. The great Texas Baptist leader, B.H. Carroll, was a consistent Calvinist in his doctrine of election, but refused to be dogmatic about particular redemption: "Pure verbal realities, however," Tom Nettles explains, "led him to protect the mysteries of the atonement, in which he saw universal benefits beyond the closures of our systems and even our present comprehension."[13] C.H. Spurgeon affirmed the doctrine of definite atonement, but he also believed, with evangelical Calvinists before and since, that "whosoever will" may come to Christ for salvation. He presented the free offer of the gospel to lost men and women with persistence and passion and so should we:

> Tell me, then, sir, whom did Christ die for? Will you answer me a question or two, and I will tell you whether He died for you. Do you want a Saviour? Do you feel that you need a Saviour? Are you this morning conscious of sin? Has the Holy Spirit taught you that you are lost? Then Christ died for you and you will be saved. Are you this morning conscious that you have no hope in the world but Christ? Do you feel that you of yourself cannot offer an atonement that can satisfy God's justice? Have you given up all confidence in yourselves? And can you say upon your bended knees, "Lord, save, or I perish"? Christ died for you.[14]

PERSONAL LEARNING ACTIVITY

The author suggests that the fifth point of Calvinism, "singular redemption," is the most controversial and least prominent in Scripture. Why does he conclude this?

_____

_____

When we are conscious that Christ is our only hope for salvation, we can be assured that His death on the cross was for us.

Falling from Grace

Before we leave our review of the doctrines of grace, we need to pause and consider how easy it is for the message of grace to be perverted. This has been a problem since the earliest days of Christianity, and it remains so today. Paul's Letter to the Galatians was written as a wake-up call to a group of believers. They were being tempted to forsake the evangelical message. Paul had proclaimed in favor of "another gospel," a

Legalism is always detrimental to our understanding and practice of God's grace.

message which mingled the grace of Christ with a theology of works-righteousness. Paul lamented the fact that these believers had been alienated from Christ: "You have fallen away from grace," he wrote (Gal. 5:4). This is a favorite proof text for those who teach that salvation can be forfeited by a truly regenerated believer, but this was not the issue that concerned Paul in this text. He was writing to Christian churches which had been founded on the teaching of grace, but were in danger of forsaking that sound doctrinal bedrock for a theology which could only lead to ruin. It is still possible for Christians to fall from grace in this sense today. Let us look at two ways in which this can happen:

1. The Labyrinth of Legalism. Labyrinth is a term that comes from ancient Greek mythology. According to legend, King Minos of Crete asked his architect to design an intricate structure with many winding passages and dead ends where he could put the Minotaur, a monstrous animal, half bull and half human. The labyrinth became a perfect prison. Once inside, there was no escape. One could go forever along its twisting paths without ever finding the exit. And so it is with legalism. *Legalism* is a distortion of the gospel which robs Christians of the freedom we have in Christ. It subverts the grace of God by taking us back into the captivity of the law. It takes our eyes off Jesus and focuses them on ourselves, filling us with pride. In the labyrinth of legalism we get lost in the maze of our own self-righteousness.

There are two kinds of legalism against which Christians must be on guard. The first is what I call "the Jesus-*and* heresy." It occurs whenever we add anything to Jesus' finished work on the cross as a necessary condition for salvation. In Galatia, Paul's opponents preached a "Jesus-and-circumcision gospel." But this kind of legalism assumes many forms: Jesus-and-water baptism, Jesus-and-good works, Jesus-and-paying our tithes, Jesus-and-Buddha, Jesus-and-the-Blessed Virgin Mary, Jesus-and-*anything!* However you interpret the details of the doctrines of grace, they all underscore the fundamental fact of Christianity: Salvation is of the Lord, and God will brook no rivals in the dispensing of His grace. Abraham Booth was a Baptist pastor who lived in England some 200 years ago. In his book, *The Reign of Grace,* he wrote:

> Divine grace disdains to be assisted in the performance of that work which peculiarly belongs to itself. … Attempts to complete what grace begins, betray our pride and offend the Lord; but cannot promote our spiritual interest. Let the reader, therefore, carefully remember, that grace is either absolutely free, or it is not at all: and, that he who professes to look for salvation by grace, either believes in his heart to be saved entirely by it, or he acts inconsistently in affairs of the greatest importance.[15]

There is also another form of legalism which robs Christians of joy in their walk with the Lord. I call it "the do's and don'ts syndrome." This kind of legalism turns Christianity into a gloomy kill-joy religion based on the strict observance of an external code of behavior, a pattern of expectations derived more from a particular culture than from the Bible itself. I grew up with this kind of legalistic Christianity. In the church of my childhood, we were quite proud of our separation from the world—from everything that even smelled worldly to us. We looked down on other Christians who dressed differently than we did, who had televisions in their homes, who sang from a different hymnal in church, whose pastor did not perspire in the pulpit as much as ours! Our pastor always removed his suit jacket when he preached. To preach with your coat on was a surefire sign of worldliness, if not liberalism! We were right to be concerned with holy living and a distinctive Christian lifestyle. But we were wrong to make ourselves the standard for all other believers. As a result, we became stodgy and inhibited in our Christian walk. Of course, we believed devoutly that salvation is by grace alone, but our lives betrayed the truth of the doctrine we professed. We were lost in the labyrinth of legalism.

We are wrong when we make ourselves the standard for all other believers.

"It is for freedom that Christ has set us free" (Gal. 5:1).

2. The Abuse of Liberty. The grace of God can be perverted in another way as well: by presuming upon it. The classic name for this attitude is *antinomianism* (from the Greek *anti,* which means "against," and *nomos,* which means "law"). Paul encountered this attitude in his day. There were some Christians who argued: Since God's grace is absolutely free and unconditional, it doesn't really matter how we live. We love to sin. God loves to forgive. So let's just go on sinning to our heart's content, knowing all the while that God's grace will always be available to cover our misdeeds. Paul was shocked at the way these believers were abusing their liberty in Christ. He exclaimed: "What shall we say, then? Shall we go on sinning so that grace may increase? By no means! We died to sin; how can we live in it any longer?" (Rom. 6:1-2).

Behind this dispute lies an important question: Does the law of God have any continuing relevance for Christians after they have been saved? We must never forget that through the redemption secured by Christ's death on the cross, believers have been liberated *from* the law. They have been accepted as righteous before God quite apart *from* the law. Legalism ignores the liberating force of this great truth. But antinomianism is another, equally dangerous deviation from the truth of the gospel. It reduces the message of salvation to cheap grace. The liberty we have in Christ is not only a freedom *from,* but also a freedom *for*—freedom for service and love. Our liberty in Christ is not a static thing, something to be admired and stroked like Silas Marner polishing his gold coins. No, true freedom is realized only through the worship and adoration of God and in selfless love for everyone created in God's image—our neighbors, coworkers, friends, family.

In this sense, the New Testament Christian, as well as the Old Testament saint, can delight in the law of God in accordance with the new nature imparted by grace alone: "Oh, how I love your law! I meditate on it all day long" (Ps. 119:97). We must never forget that not only are we saved by grace, but also we live by grace. The Scottish preacher Ralph Erskine expressed the true relationship of law and gospel in this verse:

When once the fiery law of God
Has chas'd me to the gospel-road;
Then back unto the holy law
Most kindly gospel-grace will draw.

The law most perfect still remains,
And ev'ry duty full contains:
The Gospel its perfection speaks,
And therefore gives whate'er it seeks.

A rigid master was the law,
Demanding brick, denying straw;
But when with gospel-tongue it sings,
It bids me fly, and gives me wings.[16]

It is only because "the love of God is shed abroad in our hearts by the Holy Ghost" that we are empowered to love God and to love our neighbor as well (Rom. 5:5, KJV).

---

[1]Helmut Thielicke, *The Waiting Father* (New York: Harper & Brothers, 1959), 133.

[2]David Benedict, *A General History of the Baptist Denomination in America* (Boston: Lincoln & Edmands, 1813), 456.

[3]Thomas J. Nettles, *By His Grace and for His Glory* (Grand Rapids, MI: Baker Book House, 1986), 50.

[4]n.a., "SBC president Patterson expands on various points of Calvinism" *Alabama Baptist,* 2 Dec. 1999: 11.

[5]Cornelius Plantinga, Jr., *Not the Way It's Supposed to Be* (Grand Rapids, MI: William B. Eerdmans Publishing Co., 1995), 199.

[6]Anonymous, "I Sought the Lord, and Afterward I Knew," 1878.

[7]C.H. Spurgeon, *The Metropolitan Tabernacle Pulpit* (Pasadena, TX: Pilgrim Publications, 1970), vol. XIV, 200.

[8]Robert A. Baker, *A Baptist Source Book* (Nashville, TN: Broadman Press, 1966), 208. Copyright 1966. Renewed 1994 Broadman Press. All rights reserved. Used by permission.

[9]From page 149 of *Concise Theology, A Guide to Historic Christian Beliefs* by J.I. Packer, ©1993 Foundation for Reformation. Used by permission of Tyndale House Publishers, Inc. All rights reserved.

[10]Spurgeon, *Tabernacle Pulpit,* vol. XVII, page 449 and vol. XII, page 447.

[11]*Baptist Faith and Message* tract, page 13.

[12]Charles Wesley, "And Can It Be."

[13]Nettles, *By His Grace,* 231.

[14]Charles Haddon Spurgeon, *Sermons on Sovereignty* (Pasadena, TX: Pilgrim Publications, 1990), 92.

[15]Abraham Booth, *The Reign of Grace from Its Rise to Its Consummation* (Swengel, PA: Reiner Publications, 1976), 48.

[16]Ernest Kevan, *Moral Law* (Lafayette, IN: Sovereign Grace Publishers, 1991), 74-75.

CHAPTER FIVE   Grace and the Great Commission

*The first thing that happens
after we have realized our
election to God in Christ Jesus is
the destruction of our
prejudices and our parochial
notions. … The first thing
God will do with us is to "force
through the channels
of a single heart" the interests of
the whole world.[1]*
—Oswald Chambers

In 1970, the Fellowship Baptist Church of Chickamauga, Georgia, called me to be their pastor. Chickamauga was a mill town in North Georgia, and this was my first church. I soon learned that Baptists were people of fight as well as faith! We had some terrific battles during my two-year ministry there. Should we buy a church bus? What color should we paint it? Should carpet be installed in the sanctuary? Could we put a ping-pong table in the fellowship hall so the young people would have some recreation, or would this desecrate the house of God? We fought over all these issues, but the one I remember most vividly concerned the name of the church. This became an issue after we had decided to put a sign out front with the church name on it. Brother Walker, one of our elderly deacons, insisted that the sign read "Fellowship *Missionary* Baptist Church." Everybody knew we believed in missions, but why put it on the sign? Brother Walker had moved to North Georgia from East Tennessee where it was more common for churches committed to the Great Commission to include the word *missionary* in their church name. He remembered debates with "Primitive" or "hard-shell" Baptists who were opposed to missions—at home or abroad. He didn't want us to repeat the error of those anti-missionary Baptists, and he got his way with the sign.

The attitude Brother Walker encountered as a young boy in East Tennessee is sometimes called hyper-Calvinism. In the 19th century, it was a powerful movement that ripped across the Baptist landscape leaving deep scars on many churches and associations. It is one reason why many Baptists still fear anything that smacks even slightly of Calvinism. They connect it with the memory of a movement which opposed evangelism and missions as well as Sunday Schools, theological seminaries, orphanages, and cooperative works of any kind. Although the movement no longer persists as an organized threat, some attitudes it fostered remain. Baptists may differ with one another on some details of the doctrines of grace, but there is no room in the Baptist family for one who denies Jesus' clear command, "Go and make disciples of all nations" (Matt. 28:19). Baptists are Great Commission Christians! In this chapter, we shall look briefly at the anti-missionary movement in Baptist life. We shall then profile two great Baptist heroes of the past, William Carey and Charles Haddon Spurgeon. God used both of these men in their own day to deliver Baptists (and other Christians) from the clutches of a dismal, self-focused theology. They still have much to teach us.

The Quagmire of Hyper-Calvinism

As we have seen throughout this study, it is possible to get out of theological balance by overemphasizing either the human role in conversion or the divine initiative in salvation. Radical Arminians have sometimes been guilty of the former. Their theology obscures the real meaning of grace and reduces God to a puppet on a string. Hyper-Calvinists have frequently fallen into the opposite error, so exalting God's sovereignty that human responsibility and free moral agency are denied. *Christians must ever be on guard against both extremes!* Either one is deadly to the purpose of evangelism and missions.

Article 11 of the *Baptist Faith and Message states*:

> It is the duty and privilege of every follower of Christ and of every church of the Lord Jesus Christ to endeavor to make disciples of all nations. The new birth of man's spirit by God's Holy Spirit means the birth of love for others. Missionary effort on the part of all rests thus upon a spiritual necessity of the regenerate life, and is expressly and repeatedly commanded in the teachings of Christ. It is the duty of every child of God to seek constantly to win the lost of God to Christ by personal effort and by all other methods in harmony with the gospel of Christ.[2]

It is possible to get out of theological balance by overemphasizing either the human role in conversion or the divine initiative in salvation.

Hyper-Calvinists depart from the heart of the evangelical faith in several respects. Here are five of them:

1. They teach the doctrine of eternal justification. All Calvinists believe in election—that from eternity God freely chooses in Christ those who will spend eternity with Him in heaven, and that predestines them "to be adopted as his sons [and daughters] through Jesus Christ" (Eph. 1:5). But hyper-Calvinism goes beyond this by also pushing justification back into the decrees of God. This teaching seems to completely remove a genuine human response from the process of salvation. Repentance and faith thus lose their urgency, if not their necessity. The Philadelphia *Confession of Faith,* while strongly affirming the doctrine of election, states clearly that the chosen ones "are not justified personally, until the Holy Spirit doth in due time actually apply Christ unto them."[3] This is much more in keeping with how the Bible describes the relationship between election and justification.

2. They deny the free moral agency and responsibility of sinners to repent and believe. Put otherwise, they confuse radical depravity with natural inability. This implies a deterministic view of human nature that is no different than fatalism. A proper understanding of human responsibility is essential to evangelism. The wrath of God will not be poured out on anyone because they are one of the non-elect. Instead, they will be punished for their sin and rejection of God.

3. They restrict the gospel invitation to the elect. Hyper-Calvinism teaches that since preaching is the means for the ingathering of the elect, it is wrong to preach the gospel indiscriminately to all. This view contradicts the Scriptures in which the gospel is presented as good news for all persons everywhere. Preachers do not come equipped with some sort of spiritual Geiger-counter enabling them to determine who is elect and who is not. As the conversion of the thief on the cross shows, there is no sinner so vile, no one so far gone, but that he or she may be saved by turning to Christ in repentance and faith. The gospel invitation is universal in scope.

"Whosoever shall call upon the name of the Lord shall be saved" (Rom. 10:13, KJV).

4. They teach that sinners have no warrant to believe in Christ until they feel the evidence of the Spirit's moving in their hearts. The problem with this view is that it forces lost persons to look to themselves rather than to Christ to find the proper basis for becoming a Christian. Although hyper-Calvinism usually errs on the side of utter objectivism while ignoring human responsibility, here, ironically, it plunges into the abyss of extreme subjectivity. How can lost sinners ever know whether what they are feeling is the genuine moving of the Spirit, or something else? The Bible does not say, "Wait for feelings," but rather "Trust in Jesus."

5. They deny the universal love of God. We must never deny the holiness and justice of God, which are constitutive of His divine character; but it is the love of God which draws the lost to salvation. It is wrong to play these divine attributes against one another, for they are perfectly reconciled in the one true God who is perfect in every way. But let us never forget that God does not love us because Jesus died for us, rather Jesus died for us because God loves us. Jesus loved Jerusalem and wept over it. Paul was compelled by the love of Christ to preach the gospel to everyone he met. The psalmist declared: "How excellent is thy lovingkindness, O God! *therefore* the children of men put their trust under the shadow of thy wings" (Ps. 36:7, KJV, emphasis added).

Hyper-Calvinism, then, is a perversion of true evangelical Calvinism, just as Pelagianism is a corruption of true evangelical Arminianism. In different ways, both are guilty of "falling from grace" in the sense that Paul used that expression in Galatians 5. God wants all believers to be "missionary" Christians whether we put that name on our church sign or not. Before we turn to Carey and Spurgeon, let's listen to Iain H. Murray whose study of hyper-Calvinism is one of the best to be published in recent years:

> The final conclusion has to be that when Calvinism ceases to be evangelistic, when it becomes more concerned with theory than with the salvation of men

"Whosoever will, let him take the water of life freely" (Rev. 22:17, KJV).

and women, when acceptance of doctrines seems to become more important than acceptance of Christ, then it is a system going to seed and it will invariably lose its attractive power.[4]

Into All the World: Carey's Breakthrough

The man whom we remember today as the father of modern missions, William Carey, was born in a tiny village in England in 1761. He was brought up in poverty and obscurity, with no more than a fifth- or sixth-grade education. Yet he was a genius at mastering languages and later translated the Bible into Bengali, Hindi, Sanskrit, and many other languages of India and the Far East. A sickly boy, he became a shoemaker by trade because he was not able to work outdoors in the sun. He was led to Christ by a fellow apprentice in the shoe shop and baptized as a believer in the River Nene in 1783.

William Carey had a vision for carrying the gospel into all the world.

As the young pastor of a village church, he sought to win his family and friends to Christ. But he also had a vision for carrying the gospel into all the world. This was not a popular idea in Carey's day, even among many Christians who were otherwise quite orthodox in theology. Some were in the grips of the kind of hyper-Calvinistic theology we have just reviewed. They were against human exertions of any kind in the spread of the gospel. Others held that the missionary mandate of the Great Commission was no longer applicable— it applied to the original apostles only! Since the world had already heard the gospel in the apostolic age, they reasoned, what need was there to offer it again? So pervasive was this thinking that it was reflected in an anti-missionary hymn which made the rounds in the 18th century:

Go into all the world, the Lord of old did say,
But now where He has planted thee, there thou shouldst stay.[5]

Their philosophy was simple: Just bloom where you are planted! Don't worry about those who have never heard the good news. Carey rejected this interpretation as a perversion of Jesus' command. There is no statute of limitations on the Great Commission, he said. "Go ye" means you and me—and it means here and now!

The following excerpt from *Faithful Witness: The Life and Mission of William Carey* helps to paint a picture of Carey's passion for missions.

> One of the most famous incidents in Carey's early ministry occurred when he was still a young pastor at Moulton … . At a meeting of ministers at Northampton John Ryland, Sr., called upon his colleagues to propose a topic for discussion. After a few moments of awkward silence, Carey rose and proposed for consideration, "The duty of Christians to attempt the spread of the gospel among heathen nations." Ryland, Sr. was genuinely astonished and, with a rebuking frown, thundered back, "Young man, sit down. When God pleases to convert the heathen, He will do it without your aid or mine!" A later tradition says that the elder minister referred to Carey as a "miserable enthusiast" for even raising the issue.[6]

But Carey found an able ally in his good friend and fellow pastor, Andrew Fuller. Fuller agreed with Carey completely and in 1785 he published a masterful defense of missions. His book was called *The Gospel Worthy of All Acceptation*. It contained the following six propositions:

1. Unconverted sinners are commanded, exhorted, and invited to believe in Christ for salvation.
2. Everyone is bound to receive what God reveals.
3. The gospel, though a message of pure grace, requires the obedient response of faith.
4. The lack of faith is a heinous sin which is ascribed in the Scriptures to human depravity.
5. God has threatened and inflicted the most awful punishments on sinners for their not believing on the Lord Jesus Christ.

There is no statute of limitations on the Great Commission, he said. "Go ye" means you and me—and it means here and now!

> **Carey and Fuller strongly affirmed the sovereignty of God in salvation, but, called on their fellow Christians to "exert themselves to the utmost" in fulfilling the Great Commission.**

6. The Bible requires of all persons certain spiritual exercises which are represented as their duty. These include repentance and faith no less than the requirement to love God, fear God, and glorify God. That no one can accomplish these things apart from the bestowal of the Holy Spirit is clear. Nonetheless, the obligation remains. In this respect "man's duty and God's gift" are the same thing, seen from different perspectives.[7]

Carey developed his missionary theology out of these basic insights. If sinners were *obliged* to repent and believe in Christ, as the Bible makes clear, was there not also another *obligation* to be considered? Were not Christians, themselves delivered from darkness into light, most urgently *obliged* to present the claims of Christ to those who have never heard? One of his friends, Robert Hall, put it this way: "The way to Jesus is graciously open for everyone who chooses to come to him."[8]

Carey and Fuller were attacked from both the left and the right, by Arminians and hyper-Calvinists alike. They strongly affirmed the sovereignty of God in salvation, but, far from using this doctrine as an excuse for a do-nothing approach to missions, Carey and Fuller called on their fellow Christians to "exert themselves to the utmost" in fulfilling the Great Commission. The God who predestined the salvation of the elect, they reasoned, also predestined the means by which they would be saved. The "means" God had chosen included the sending of missionaries, the raising up of evangelists, and the preaching of the gospel in every corner of the world.

In 1792 Carey published his ideas about missions in a little booklet which became the manifesto of the modern missionary movement. Its title is worthy of quoting in full: "An Enquiry into the Obligations of Christians, to use Means for the Conversion of the Heathens, in which the Religious State of the Different Nations of the World, the Success of Former Undertakings, and the Practicability of Further Undertakings, are Considered," by William Carey. Carey summed up his plan in four words:

1. Pray: This is something all Christians can do and ought to do, Carey said. Fervent and united prayer is the divinely appointed prerequisite for a revival of the missionary spirit.

2. Plan: Carey combined his idealism of absolute commitment with the most practical realism possible. God honors wise planning in missions no less than in any other area of His kingdom's work. Carey the shoemaker never lost his common sense, no-nonsense approach to missions.

3. Give: Every Christian has something to offer, Carey said. If all Christians would tithe their income, he observed, there would be an abundance of resources to support the ministry of the gospel at home as well as to sponsor the cause of Christ abroad. There should be special collections even if it is only one penny per week, and sacrificial giving by all.

4. Go: Carey volunteered himself. He said to his friends, "I will go down but remember you must hold the ropes."[9] Fuller and a few other friends said they would be the rope-holders. They formed the first missionary society and took up the first missionary offering for the expressed purpose of sending the gospel to those who had never heard the name of Jesus. They were evangelical Calvinists, and they called their group the "Particular Baptist Society for the Propagation of the Gospel Amongst the Heathen."

And so, on June 13, 1793, William Carey, his wife, Dorothy, and their four children including a nursing infant, sailed from England on a Danish ship headed for India. No one on board that ship would ever see his or her native homeland again. Carey served for 41 years in India without ever coming home on furlough. During those decades, he blazed a trail that thousands of others have since followed. Carey's missionary legacy is astounding even today: He translated the Scriptures, ran a publishing house, founded a college, organized scores of schools, planted numerous churches, sent out hundreds of Indian evangelists, worked tirelessly for human rights including the abolition of both slavery and the horrible practice of widow-burning, worked for prison reform, and more. What was the secret of his success?

> **Prayer is the divinely appointed prerequisite for a revival of the missionary spirit.**

Missions is rooted in the gracious, eternal purpose of the triune God.

Carey knew that Christian missions was rooted in the gracious, eternal purpose of the triune God—the Father, the Son, and the Holy Spirit—to call unto Himself a redeemed people out of the fallen race of humankind. It was not in spite of, but rather because of, his belief in the greatness of God and His divine purpose that Carey was willing to venture all to proclaim the gospel in the far corners of the world. In the midst of great discouragement and even depression, Carey was convinced that God's purpose could not fail. He preached the gospel with compassion but without compromise, because he sensed so keenly the eternal destiny of every person he met. He shuddered to think of the dire consequences of spurning Christ's invitation to eternal life.

Time and again Carey was forced to learn the lesson of trusting in God to bring His purpose to fulfillment. He entered India as an illegal alien without a passport. He struggled as a farmer to eke out a living for his family. There were family tragedies—his son Peter died, his wife, Dorothy, went mad. There was opposition back home and some of the "rope-holders" let go; there was jealousy from fellow workers and controversy with political leaders. What sustained Carey through all these "toils and snares"? He was resourceful and tenacious, to be sure, but this is not what kept him focused on the goal which had led him to India in the first place. No, his difficulties drove him into the arms of his sovereign Lord. Here he found comfort and strength, as this entry from his diary reveals: "I feel that it is good to commit my soul, my body, and my all, into the hands of God. Then the world appears little, the promises great, and God an all-sufficient portion."[10]

Back in England when Carey was still struggling with the decision to go to India, he visited John Newton, famous author of "Amazing Grace" who was then a pastor in London. Newton prayed with Carey and offered this counsel: All that is memorable in the annals of history, he said, take place according to God's plan. Unless God is in this work, all your efforts of utmost strength and wisdom will come to naught. But when God does have a work to accomplish and His time has come, nothing in heaven or upon earth can stand in His way. He is the Lord God Almighty, and His works are great and marvelous! To the end of his life, Carey remembered Newton's words. They brought him great comfort and strength when there were few "visible results" to show for his labors.

Not long before his visit with Newton, Carey had been asked to preach the principal sermon at the annual meeting of his local Baptist association. He took his text from Isaiah 54:2-4: "Enlarge the place of thy tent, and let them stretch forth the curtains of thine habitations: spare not, lengthen thy cords, and strengthen thy stakes; For thou shalt break forth on the right hand and on the left; and thy seed shall inherit the Gentiles, and make the desolate cities to be inhabited. Fear not; for thou shalt not be ashamed" (KJV). Carey summarized his message in two simple commands; together they became the watchwords of the modern missionary movement: "Expect great things *from* God. Attempt great things *for* God."[11]

"Expect great things from God. Attempt great things for God."
–William Carey

When kept together, and stated in the right order, these two simple imperatives from Carey reflect the right biblical balance between an emphasis on the sovereignty of God and the missionary mandate of the church. Arminianism tends to place the "attempting" before the "expecting." This is to get the cart before the horse: It invariably leads to a prayerless activism which ends in frustrated exhaustion. Hyper-Calvinists, on the other hand, are big on "expecting," but they never get around to "attempting." They fail to see that the fruit of Christian faith is Christian enterprise; that we are called to be, in the daring language of Paul himself, nothing less than "labourers together with God" (1 Cor. 3:9, KJV). For sure, God is never at our beck and call, but we *are* at His beck and call. Today God still calls us, as He called Carey and the Baptists of his day, to boldness in missions. He wants us to be bold expecters and bold attempters! Looking back on Carey's message, Andrew Fuller had this to say: "I feel the use of his sermon to this day. Let us pray much, hope much, expect much, labor much; an eternal weight of glory awaits us!"[12]

PERSONAL LEARNING ACTIVITY

William Carey's words, "Expect great things from God. Attempt great things for God," became the watchword for the modern missionary movement. Why is it important that this statement be kept together and stated as is?

_____

_____

Both William Carey and Charles Haddon Spurgeon were men of compassion and love.

The Gospel Freely Offered to All: Spurgeon's Passion

William Carey died in India on June 9, 1834. As he had requested, these words from a hymn by Isaac Watts were inscribed on the stone slab which marked his grave: "A wretched, poor, and helpless worm, On thy kind arms I fall."[13] Exactly 10 days after Carey died, Charles Haddon Spurgeon was born in a thatched cottage in the small village of Kelvedon in Essex. In many ways these two giants of Baptist history were very different: Carey, the humble shoemaker turned missionary pioneer; Spurgeon, the renowned pastor and prince of preachers. Carey was shy and retiring; Spurgeon was a volcano of a personality, bursting with energy. Yet both men drank deeply from the wells of divine grace. Both were committed unflinchingly to the sovereignty of God, but neither could abide the lifeless traditionalism which stifled the cause to evangelism. Both were men of compassion and love. They proclaimed a holistic gospel addressed to living persons, soul and body, in all of their broken humanity and need for wholeness. In their own day, and since then, their influence and witness has extended far beyond the bounds of the Baptist family. Though they are long dead, like Abel, they still speak (see Heb. 11:4). Their lives still glitter with grace.

Carey's mission to India inspired many others to carry the good news of Christ into all the world—David Livingstone in

Africa, Henry Martyn in Persia, Lottie Moon and Hudson Taylor in China. But the movement for world evangelization also provoked a revival of the attitude Carey had confronted as a young pastor in England. Matthew 28:19-20 again became a battleground. Some saw it as an obscure text with little relevance for the contemporary church. Others found in it the marching orders for every Christian. Spurgeon belonged enthusiastically to the latter group. He spoke strongly against those who ignored the clear meaning of Jesus' words:

Matthew 28:19-20 contains the marching orders for every Christian.

> I have met with some brethren who have tried to read the Bible the wrong way upwards. They have said, "God has a purpose which is certain to be fulfilled, therefore we will not budge an inch. All power is in the hands of Christ, therefore we will sit still"; but that is not Christ's way of reading the passage. It is, "All power is given unto me, *therefore go ye*, and do something."[14]... The lazy-bones of our orthodox churches cry, "God will do his own work"; and then they look out the softest pillow they can find, and put it under their heads, and say, "The eternal purposes will be carried out: God will be glorified." That is all very fine talk, but it can be used with the most mischievous design. You can make opium out of it, which will lull you into a deep and dreadful slumber, and prevent your being of any kind of use at all.[15]

Spurgeon was a mega-church pastor before mega-churches were cool. In 40 years of ministry, Spurgeon preached to some 10 million people. Each week thousands crowded into the Metropolitan Tabernacle in London. On Sunday nights the crowds grew so large that Spurgeon asked his own members to stay at home or gather for prayer in other places so that the throngs of visitors could find a seat! Spurgeon appealed to them all—from paupers and street urchins to statesmen and peers of the realm. On one occasion, Queen Victoria herself put on a disguise and came to the Tabernacle.

> We need a revival of the kind of God-intoxicated, grace-filled preaching that marked Spurgeon's ministry.

Spurgeon was unique. It would be foolish for any pastor to try to imitate him today. But we do need a revival of the kind of God-intoxicated, grace-filled preaching that marked his ministry. What was Spurgeon's preaching like? It was biblical, trinitarian, promiscuous, urgent, and compassionate.

1. Biblical: Spurgeon lived in a day when arguing about the Bible and theology was much in vogue. He was aware of these currents of thought, but they seldom showed up in his preaching. He knew that it was futile to try to prove God by an intellectual demonstration. Spurgeon knew that God had revealed His will in Holy Scripture and that preaching had to be an exposition of the Bible. The preacher must speak from the Bible and not just about it. His job is not to give a learned discourse on history, apologetics, ethics, current events, or anything else, but rather to declare an unequivocal "Thus saith the Lord." I like the story of the little eight-year-old boy who was taken to hear Spurgeon preach. His father told him that he was about to hear the greatest preacher in the world. When it was over, the boy said, "I know how to be the greatest preacher in the world." "How?" asked his father. "Why, just pick out a nice chapter in the Bible, and tell just what is in it so that everybody can understand you, and nothing more."[16]

2. Trinitarian: Because Spurgeon's preaching was so thoroughly biblical, it was also inherently trinitarian. He never ceased to magnify the one God who is Father, Son, and Holy Spirit, the God of creation, redemption, and consummation. Spurgeon knew, of course, that the heart of the gospel was Jesus Christ and he never tired of lifting Him up. He once said, "A Christless gospel is no gospel and a Christless discourse is the cause of merriment to devils. … Jesus, Jesus, Jesus, only have we laboured to extol."[17] But which Jesus did Spurgeon preach? If Jesus were not the divine Son of God, co-eternal with the Father and the Holy Spirit, His work on the cross would have had no more saving value than the death of Socrates. Spurgeon frequently began his sermons with prayers which showed the deep trinitarian structure of his understanding of the Christian life. In these prayers he gave all honor and glory to the one God who made heaven and earth. He would confess that God has revealed Himself in the Trinity of His sacred persons. He praised the glorious Father, as the covenant God of Israel; the gracious Son as the Redeemer of His people; and the Holy Ghost as the author of sanctification. He expressed everlasting praise to God for the gospel of free grace proclaimed unto all through Jesus Christ our Lord.

We can get out of balance by overemphasizing one of the divine Persons to the exclusion of the other two. Unitarianism proclaims "the Fatherhood of God and the brotherhood of man" but reduces Jesus to a pious teacher and the Holy Spirit to an impersonal idea. Some "Jesus only" denominations collapse the Trinity into Christ, while certain pentecostal and charismatic churches so exalt the Spirit that the Father and the Son are ignored. Spurgeon knew that the gospel of free grace requires us to pay equal attention to all three persons of the Holy Trinity in the unity of their redeeming work.

3. Promiscuous: The word *promiscuous* has a very negative meaning as we so often use it today. It refers to someone who is immoral and carries on illicit affairs with many persons. But the word itself means simply "different elements mixed or mingled together, indiscriminate." In this sense, Spurgeon's preaching was *promiscuous* in its scope. He believed that the good news of the gospel was intended to be proclaimed indiscriminately to all persons everywhere.

As we have seen, this flew in the face of the hyper-Calvinistic practice of addressing the claims of the gospel to the elect only. Spurgeon pointed out that in the Bible the gospel was preached to human beings not as elect or non-elect, but simply as sinners in need of redemption. In his sermon on Mars Hill, Paul was emphatic that God "commands all people everywhere to repent" (Acts 17:30). And he linked this universal call for repentance with the future judgment God has appointed for the whole world (see Acts 17:31). Like Carey before him, Spurgeon believed that the Great Commission was universal in its outreach. We are to preach the gospel to every creature, not merely to those already

In the Bible the gospel was preached to human beings not as elect or non-elect, but simply as sinners in need of redemption.

regenerated, or to those we suppose may be in the number of the elect. Such speculation is both foolish and dangerous.

One of Spurgeon's favorite Bible verses was John 6:37. Like Carey's "Expect great things, attempt great things," this verse holds divine sovereignty and human responsibility together in beautiful equipoise. Spurgeon preached many sermons from this text. Here is a sample from one of them:

> "Him that cometh to me I will in no wise cast out." ... "Him that cometh to me:" that is the character. The man may have been guilty of an atrocious sin, too black for mention; but if he comes to Christ he shall not be cast out. ... I cannot tell what kind of persons may have come into this Hall to-night; but if burglars, murderers, and dynamite-men were here, I would still bid them come to Christ, for he will not cast them out. ... No limit is set to the extent of sin: any "him" in all the world—any blaspheming, devilish "him" that comes to Christ shall be welcomed. I use strong words that I may open wide the gate of mercy. Any "him" that comes to Christ—though he come from slum or taproom, betting-ring or gambling-hall, prison or brothel—Jesus will in no wise cast out.[18]

4. Urgent: For Spurgeon a sermon was not a lecture but a summons, divinely sent, with eternal consequences in the balance. This is why he preached with an urgency and passion that was riveting to his hearers. In Spurgeon's day, there were those who felt the preacher's task was done once he had presented the bare facts of the gospel. Spurgeon knew that this way of thinking did not mesh with the pattern of apostolic preaching in the Bible. Why did Paul say that "Christ's love compels [constraineth, KJV] us" (2 Cor. 5:14)? Why did he consider his life worth nothing? Why did he weep night and day as he presented the gospel to the people of Ephesus (see Acts 20:31)? The true presentation of the gospel must be more than the dispensing of information. It must be an invitation.

"Him that cometh to me I will in no wise cast out" *(John 6:37).*

This invitation is not like inviting someone to go to a concert or to go bowling. This invitation comes not from the preacher, but from God. This invitation cannot be equated with walking the aisle or shaking the pastor's hand, though God can and does use such public expressions to draw lost sinners unto Himself. This invitation is extended by Jesus Himself. It comes from the Scriptures through the preacher. It is extended by the Holy Spirit who convicts the sinner and draws him or her to the fountain of grace.

5. Compassionate: The Dutch theologian Herman Bavinck wrote that the gospel is "so powerful that it cannot be conquered, and yet so loving that it excludes all force."[19] This is also an apt description of Spurgeon's preaching. It was filled with compassion, tenderheartedness, and a constant appeal to the love of God. Those who restrict the love of God only to the elect are impugning an essential element of His divine character. Only three times in the Bible is God directly equated with some particular reality other than one of His personal names: "God is light" (1 John 1:5); "God is a consuming fire" (Heb. 12:29); and "God is love" (1 John 4:16).

Spurgeon's heart was ablaze with the love of God and this was evident in his love for the lost.

> "We win by love," says Spurgeon. "We win hearts for Jesus by love, by sympathy with their sorrows, by anxiety lest they should perish, by pleading with God for them with all our hearts that they would not be left to die unsaved, by pleading with them for God that, for their own sake, they would seek mercy and find grace."[20]

"God is love" (1 John 4:16).

These were not merely words from the pulpit. They reflected a lifestyle of compassion and neighborly love which took with utmost seriousness every person created in the image of God. Long before the term *social ministry* was in vogue, Spurgeon reached out with the love of Jesus to orphans and unwanted children, to women of the gutter, to the nameless nobodies who crowded the streets of victorian London. The demands of his ministry were staggering, but he was never too busy to counsel with the troubled soul, to pray with the sick, to visit the bereaved.

Acts of love and mercy authenticate preaching about God's grace.

Such acts of mercy gave authenticity to his preaching about grace. No one has ever accused Spurgeon of ignoring theology or being soft on doctrine. But he was wise enough to know that doctrine alone is not enough: "When love dies orthodox doctrine becomes a corpse, a powerless formalism. Adhesion to the truth sours into bigotry when the sweetness and light of love to Jesus depart. ... Lose love, lose all."[21]

PERSONAL LEARNING ACTIVITY

About Spurgeon, it was said that "acts of mercy gave authenticity to his preaching about grace." How do you authenticate grace in your world?

_____

How can you authenticate grace in your church?

_____

How can you authenticate grace in your family?

_____

Learning from the Past

It has been more than 100 years since Spurgeon died, and more than 200 years since Carey's mission to India. Today the Christian world stands again at a critical juncture in the fulfillment of the Great Commission. At Beeson Divinity School, there is a digital world population clock which electronically ticks out the number of people on earth second by second, number by number. It is a chilling experience to stand in front of that clock and see the rapidly changing numbers, each one representing a soul which will spend eternity either with God or separated from Him. Of the more than six billion persons on earth, nearly two billion of them have never heard the name of Jesus. Carey burned with compassion for the lost world, for those who were perishing without Christ. He knew that the grace of God was not the private possession of the frozen chosen, the cozy elect. It was good news, the best news possible, amazing news of a gracious God who loved so deeply that in His absolute freedom and sovereignty, He chose to show mercy rather than execute justice (which He may well have done by right) against guilty sinners. Carey went to India to proclaim by word and deed this glorious gospel—the good news of a God who brings sinners from unimaginable misery into unimaginable glory *sola gratia,* "by grace alone!" Today, more than anything else, the church of Jesus Christ needs a fresh vision of Carey's God—a full-sized God, eternal, transcendent, holy, filled with compassion—sovereignly working by His Spirit to call unto Himself a people out of every nation, kindred, tribe, and language group on earth. Only such a vision, born of repentance, prayer, and self-denial, can inspire a Carey-like faith in this new generation.

As Spurgeon grew older, his battle for gospel preaching intensified. He became embroiled in a major theological dispute known as the Down Grade Controversy. This was brought about by the unwarranted concessions some Christian leaders were making to the rising tide of liberal theology. Fundamental issues of the historic Christian faith were under attack from those who no longer found them "relevant" to the needs of the church. The person and work of Christ was denigrated, and the total truthfulness of Scripture was denied. Jesus' substitutionary atonement was relegated to the dustbin of theory. Spurgeon resisted this doctrinal laxity and error. He endeavored to stave off "the boiling mudshowers of modern heresy,"[23] which were beginning to descend on church life in his day. In hyper-Calvinism, Spurgeon had encountered a rationalism of the right, a theology so enthralled with the power of God that it lost sight of His love.

Of the more than six billion persons on earth, nearly two billion of them have never heard the name of Jesus for the first time.

Now, in the Down Grade Controversy he came face-to-face with a rationalism of the left, an anti-supernaturalist ideology that eviscerated the heart of the gospel itself.

Confronted with this new challenge, Spurgeon looked back on some of the earlier disputes between Calvinists and Arminians and he saw them in a different light: "We used to debate upon particular and general redemption, but now men question whether there is any redemption at all worthy of the name."[23] To the end of his life, Spurgeon continued to preach both the sovereignty of God in salvation and the universal love of God for the lost. God did not create human beings to be damned. If they are damned (and Spurgeon believed in an actual, eternal hell), their damnation is all of them. But if they are saved, their salvation is all of God. Some people accused Spurgeon of being a rigid Calvinist because he did believe and preach the doctrines of grace. Others called him an Arminian because he stressed human responsibility and preached the gospel indiscriminately to all.

Both divine sovereignty and human responsibility are biblical and evangelical truths, which must be held in tension if the gospel is to be proclaimed in its purity and urgency.

Was Spurgeon really inconsistent? No more or less so than the Bible itself. The theology of grace in Christian history oscillates between the poles of divine sovereignty and human responsibility. Both are biblical and evangelical truths, which must be held in tension if the gospel is to be proclaimed in its purity and urgency. Spurgeon was willing to live with that tension knowing that one day in heaven, if we need to know how this deep mystery is resolved in God's own mind, He will reveal it to us in His own time and in His own way. In one of his last sermons at the Metropolitan Tabernacle, Spurgeon looked back over the years of his ministry and remarked:

> I have endeavored, in my ministry, to preach to you, not a part of the truth, but the whole counsel of God; but I cannot harmonize it, nor am I anxious to do so. I am sure all truth is harmonious, and *to my ear* the harmony is clear enough; but I cannot give you a complete score of the music, or mark the harmonies on the gamut, I must leave the Chief Musician to do that.[24]

PERSONAL LEARNING ACTIVITY

Spurgeon preached both the sovereignty of God and salvation and the universal love of God for the lost. How was he able to reconcile these two great truths?

_____

_____

In heaven, if we need to know how the deep mystery of God's sovereignty and human freedom is resolved in God's own mind, He will reveal it to us in His own time and in His own way.

[1]Oswald Chambers, *My Utmost for His Highest* (Westwood, NJ: Barbour and Company, Inc., 1935), 195.

[2]Robert A. Baker, *A Baptist Source Book* (Nashville, TN: Broadman Press, 1966), 209. Copyright 1966. Renewed 1994 Broadman Press. All rights reserved. Used by permission.

[3]John Broadus, Timothy and Denise George, eds., *Baptist Confessions, Covenants, and Catechisms* (Nashville, Tenn., Broadman & Holman Publishers, 1996), 70. ©1996 by Broadman & Holman. Used by permission.

[4]Iain H. Murray, *Spurgeon v. Hyper-Calvinism* (Carlisle, PA: The Banner of Truth Trust, 1995), 120.

[5]n.a., from eighteenth-century hymn as quoted in Timothy George, *Faithful Witness: The Life and Mission of William Carey* (Birmingham, AL: New Hope, 1991), 39.

[6]Ibid., 53.

[7]As quoted in *Faithful Witness,* 56-57.

[8]Ibid., 57.

[9]Ibid., 74.

[10]Ibid., 104.

[11]Ibid., 32.

[12]Ibid., 33.

[13]Ibid., 168.

[14]C.H. Spurgeon, *The Metropolitan Tabernacle Pulpit* (Pasadena, TX: Pilgrim Publications, 1976), vol. XLII, 234.

[15]Spurgeon, *Tabernacle Pulpit,* vol. XXX, 630.

[16]As quoted in Lewis A. Drummond, *Spurgeon: Prince of Preachers* (Grand Rapids, MI: Kregel Publications, 1992), 301.

[17]Ibid., 290.

[18]Spurgeon, *Tabernacle Pulpit,* vol. XXX, 54-55.

[19]As quoted in Anthony A. Hoekema, *Saved by Grace* (Grand Rapids, MI: William B. Eerdmans Publishing Co., 1989), 105.

[20]Murray, *Spurgeon v. Hyper-Calvinism,* 94.

[21]Spurgeon, *Tabernacle Pulpit,* vol. XXXII, 580-581.

[22]As quoted in Timothy George and David Dockery, eds., *Baptist Theologians* (Nashville, TN: Broadman Press, 1990), 95.

[23]C.H. Spurgeon, *An All-Round Ministry* (Carlisle, PA: The Banner of Truth Trust, 1900), 285.

[24]Spurgeon, *Tabernacle Pulpit,* vol. LII, 101.

CHAPTER SIX

Living by Grace

I feel that, if I could live a thousand lives, I would like to live them all for Christ, and I should even then feel that they were all too little a return for his great love to me.[1]
—Charles Haddon Spurgeon

God's grace is always purposeful, never capricious or haphazard. God has a purpose for all believers who have been saved by grace. What is that purpose? It is this: that they should "be conformed to the likeness of his Son" (Rom. 8:29). J.B. Phillips translates that verse in this way: "God, in his fore-knowledge, chose them to bear the family likeness of his Son, that he might be the eldest of a family of many brothers." This means that grace is operative in the life of the believer not only at the moment of conversion but all the way through our Christian experience. Not only are we saved by grace, we are meant to live by grace too.

Paul had this same thought in mind when writing to the Christians in Galatia. In a startling image, he compared his ministry among them to a mother undergoing again the pains of childbirth: "until Christ is formed in you" (Gal. 4:19). The Greek word for "be formed in you" is *morphoó,* a medical term for the growth of a fetus into an infant. Paul was deeply concerned about these new believers. He did not want them to suffer a spiritual miscarriage but desired instead that they make their calling and election sure. Paul assumed that they had indeed been born again, that Christ is in them already. But Christ must continue to be formed in them just as they are being formed in Him. They need to grow in grace, in Christlikeness. They need to experience more and more "the life of God in the soul of man," as the title of Henry Scougal's classic book on spirituality puts it. The great evangelist George Whitefield understood this when he wrote in his journal: "God soon showed me ... that 'true religion was union of the soul with God, and Christ formed within us.'"[2]

In this concluding chapter, we are going to look at several questions which have arisen throughout this study on what it means to live by grace. Before we begin this review, however, let's look briefly at some of the ground we have covered already. In chapter 1 we began our study by defining *grace* as God's free and sovereign favor to ill-deserving sinners. We also saw how grace is consistent with the character of God Himself and how it fills every aspect of His long-range plan of salvation. In chapter 2 we explored the theme of divine providence. We saw how God governs the course of history both by direct intervention and through the freely chosen acts of human beings created in His image. We also saw how God uses suffering and tragedy as occasions to display His glory. This principle is evident throughout the Bible, but nowhere more clearly than in the event of Jesus' crucifixion where God used the most horrible event imaginable, the brutalizing death of His own Son, to fulfill His perfect plan of redemption.

Next, in chapter 3, we looked at some of the debates Christians have carried on among themselves about the nature of grace and how it works in relation to human freedom. We found Augustine's thoughts very helpful on this subject, though we could not follow his theology in every detail. We also considered how Christians who hold differing views on the details of predestination may nonetheless stand united in Christ and work together in sharing the gospel with the lost. In chapter 4 we reviewed some of the ways the doctrines of grace have been seen historically and we glanced briefly at a couple of serious deviations from the biblical doctrine of grace—legalism and antinomianism. In chapter 5 we looked at the meaning of grace in relation to the Great Commission. We pointed out how those who use God's grace as an excuse for laziness and inaction are really perverters of the good news itself. We saw how William Carey overcame obstinate opposition to carry the gospel into all the world. And we also looked at Charles Haddon Spurgeon, the prince of preachers, who proclaimed God's illimitable love to "whosoever will" while never denying God's sovereign grace in the salvation of every sinner who comes to Christ. Let's look now at some of the questions that have arisen in our study.

The Bible says that we are to "grow in the grace and knowledge of our Lord and Savior Jesus Christ" (2 Pet. 3:18).

What's So Amazing About Grace?

This question is the title of a book written by Philip Yancey several years ago. It suggests that, for many people, there is really nothing about grace sufficiently amazing to justify that adjective. Sadly, this is true for thousands of folks, including many who have grown up around the church. They have grown up with the language of grace and the music of grace, but their hearts have grown hardened to the true reality of grace. They suffer from grace-inflation. God's love and mercy no longer amaze, astound, and shatter. They have become deaf to grace's melodies and blind to its glories. For people like this, it may take a tragedy or an emergency to shatter the myth of self-sufficiency with which they have "protected" themselves from the wooings of grace. When people are flat on their backs, they can only look up. In such a moment, their need for God may be revealed and they will see, perhaps for the first time, three amazing facts about grace.

1. It's undeserved! In our modern industrialized societies, almost everything is based on what might be called "a theology of grabs." If you want to get ahead in business, then you must claw your way to the top of the organization. If you want to succeed in politics, you'd better grab the initiative from your opponent—destroying him in the process if possible. Feminism says to women, "grab the power from the men." Even children are told that they may sue their parents and grab authority for themselves. Many people carry this same "theology of grabs" into the spiritual realm assuming that they can relate to God on a quid pro quo basis. But the Bible tells another story. It says that God is too great and holy, and that our sins are too deep and dark, to allow this kind of bargaining at the barricade of salvation.

Jesus told a parable about a man who owned a vineyard (see Matt. 20:1-16). He went out early one morning and hired some laborers to work in his field. Around noontime he brought on a second shift; then again, right before closing, he hired a few more stragglers and put them to work. At the end of the day, everyone was paid the same amount! Those who

> Many people have grown up with the language of grace and the music of grace, but their hearts have grown hardened to the true reality of grace.

had toiled all day in the sun were furious. "We deserve much more than these Johnny-come-lately's!" they might have exclaimed in today's terminology. They were amazed, and quite upset, at the generosity of the owner toward these ill-deserving workers. The disgruntled workers' argument makes perfect sense in "the kingdom of grabs," but not in the kingdom of grace. Here we learn that God does not play by our rules. The vineyard is His. The fact that He calls us at all is a matter of sheer grace, His undeserved favor. If God blesses us with good things, including salvation, it is not because of the hours worked, the effort expended, the merits earned. It is all grace, grace undeserved

2. It's unexpected! The grouchy workers in Jesus' parable expected one thing and got something else. In Ezekiel 37, God shows the prophet a valley of dry bones, the desiccated remnants of a once great army. "Can these bones live?" the Lord asks Ezekiel. To which the prophet replies, "O sovereign Lord, you alone know" (v. 3). At God's command, Ezekiel speaks His Word. The Spirit blows across the valley. The unexpected, the impossible, happens: the army comes to life again!

The story of Racehoss Sample illustrates how God's grace works unexpectedly in human lives. Racehoss was the son of Big Emma, a Texas prostitute who beat and abused her unwanted child until he ran away from home at age 11. He lived like a bum until he joined the army. Soon he went AWOL and was eventually sentenced to 30 years in the Texas State Penitentiary for assault and battery. He was so rough that he had to be placed in solitary confinement, a filthy pit of absolute darkness. In this hellhole, he was reduced to the level of an animal groveling for the morsels of food thrown down to him from time to time. In the midst of desperation, he cried one day: "Help me God! Help meeeee!" Here is how he described what happened next:

A ray of light between my fingers. Slowly uncovering my face, the whole cell was illuminated like a 40-watt bulb turned on. The soft light soothed me and I no longer was

Augustus Toplady expressed the undeserved nature of God's love for us in his classic hymn, "Rock of Ages":

Not the labors of my hands
Can fulfill Thy law's demands;
Could my zeal no respite know,
Could my tears forever flow,
All for sin could not atone;
Thou must save
and Thou alone.[3]

afraid. Engulfed by a presence, I felt it reassuring me. It comforted me … I breathed freely. I had never felt such well being, so good, in all my life. Safe. Loved.

The voice within talked through the pit of my belly. "You are not an animal. You are a human being." And "Don't you worry about a thing. But you must tell them about me."

After that, God was real. He found me in the abyss of the burning hell, uplifted and fed my hungry soul, and breathed new life into my nostrils.[4]

> **God's grace can break through the most impenetrable barriers in the most unexpected manner.**

On January 12, 1972, Racehoss walked out of prison a free man and a new creation in Christ. He later served as a probation officer and was named the Outstanding Crime Prevention Citizen of Texas in 1981. Eventually he received a full pardon. The story of Racehoss Sample is unique. His conversion to Christ was unusual and dramatic. But it reminds us that God's grace can break through the most impenetrable barriers.

3. It's inexplicable! Several times in this study we have encountered the word *mystery*. A mystery is something we know to be true because God has revealed it to be so in His Word, but we cannot explain it or account for it in terms of our human rationality and logic. God's grace is inexplicable in this way. This is why Paul's theology turns into doxology at the end of Romans 11. After dealing extensively with the profound issues of predestination and grace, he throws up his hands, as it were, and exclaims:

Frankly, I stand amazed at the unfathomable complexity of God's wisdom and God's knowledge. How could man ever understand his reasons for action, or explain his methods of working? … For of him, and through him, and unto him, are all things. To him be the glory for ever, amen! (Rom. 11:30,36, Phillips).

PERSONAL LEARNING ACTIVITY

The author reminds us that God's grace can break through the most impenetrable barriers in the most unexpected manner. How have you experienced such a miraculous event as this? Describe it below.

_____

_____

Why Talk About Predestination?

If we will never be able to fully explain the mystery of divine grace this side of heaven, then why should we talk about such thorny issues as predestination, God's eternal decrees, and the like? There are two answers to this question. It is right to study this doctrine because it is biblically significant and because it is pastorally relevant.

Several years ago I visited Thomas Jefferson's famous home, Monticello. While touring his library, we were shown a copy of Jefferson's New Testament. The curator held it up to let us see how it was full of holes. Jefferson had gone through with a penknife and cut out all the references that offended him, all the verses about God's wrath, hell, judgment, and so forth. While no Bible-believing Christian would be so impudent as Jefferson in actually deleting a part of God's Word, in reality we are guilty of a similar offense when we deliberately ignore any portion of what God has revealed to us in Scripture. We are not free to ignore the doctrine of predestination simply because we do not like it, cannot understand it, or do not see how it can be squared with a particular philosophical understanding of reality. If we affirm the verbal inspiration of the Bible, as we should, then we know that God has wasted no words in revealing His will to us. There are many doctrinal truths we may not be able to understand perfectly in this life, but God has revealed them to us for a

> It is right to study this doctrine because it is biblically significant and because it is pastorally relevant.

purpose. It is our duty to rightly divide the Word of truth so that we may understand them more fully and thus love and serve God more faithfully until in heaven we shall see "face to face" (1 Cor. 13:12).

The doctrine of grace is not only biblically significant, it's pastorally relevant. Paul discovered that God's grace was sufficient in the extremities of his life, and so it has been for Christians through the ages. Some years ago a good friend stopped by my office to share with me the shattering news he had just received: his wife was leaving him and their children for another man. I didn't know how to respond or what to say. But I remember mumbling, "I love you, and there is grace." More recently, my colleague Lewis Drummond, after a serious bout with cancer, said to me: "Timothy, I have preached about grace all my life, but now I know its meaning more deeply than I ever have before. I have been to the bottom, and I can tell you that it is solid." Both of these friends learned through experience the powerful promise God made to Israel long ago: "Fear not, for I have redeemed you; I have summoned you by name; you are mine. When you pass through the waters, I will be with you … when you walk through the fire, you will not be burned" (Isa. 43:1-2).

> "Prayer must be built on the foundation of the sovereignty and character of God."[5]
> –T.W. Hunt

Why Should We Pray?

All Christians pray. We begin our walk with God by crying out: "Lord, be merciful to me a sinner." We grow step-by-step in our relationship with God as our hearts become centered on Him. We hear Him speak to us by His Spirit through the Scriptures, and we respond in petition, intercession, confession and praise. We know that God wants us to pray and that He hears and responds to us. A Christian who does not pray is like a bird that cannot fly or a fire that does not burn.

T.W. Hunt has said that "prayer must be built on the foundation of the sovereignty and character of God."[5] We have no "right" to approach God on our own, apart from Christ, for our sins have placed an unbridgeable gulf between Him and us. We dare to come to the throne of grace only because we are invited to do so by the God who is limitless in His love as well as awesome in His holiness. Still, though, the question persists: If God is truly omniscient, knowing everything that will happen before it occurs, why should we pray? What difference do our prayers make? Wouldn't everything turn out just the same if we never prayed at all? Doesn't God's initiative in loving, choosing, redeeming, calling and preserving His children invalidate their need to respond to Him in prayer?

These questions have been asked through the ages, and they deserve a straightforward response. That response is simple: God foreknows and chooses the means as well as the end, and our prayers are one of the foreordained means He has chosen to bring to pass what He has sovereignly intended. Again, we may not be able to explain perfectly how our prayers and God's purpose work together compatibly to accomplish what God of His own "good pleasure" has determined, but that this is so we can have no doubt for it is clearly attested in Scripture (Luke 12:32, NKJV).

Second Corinthians 1:8-11 is one of many passages where this principle is clearly set forth. In these verses, Paul told the believers in Corinth about terrible hardships and sufferings he endured in his missionary travels. Some of these were so severe that he did not think he would survive. But he saw God's purpose and plan behind it all: "But this happened that we might not rely on ourselves but on God, who raises the dead" (v. 9). In the meantime, the Lord delivered him from this peril and, Paul believed, continued to sustain him and enabled him to proclaim the gospel to others. But how would God do this? Paul's answer was clear: "He will continue to deliver us, *as you help us by your prayers.* Then many will give thanks on our behalf for the gracious favor granted us in answer to the prayers of many" (vv. 10-11, emphasis added). The Corinthian Christians were praying for Paul; God used their prayers for Him to rescue him from imminent danger.

When we pray for missionaries we have never seen, some of whom are serving Christ in faraway places, we should remember that God uses our prayers to strengthen and

God uses our prayers to strengthen and help others.

God still works through the prayers of His people.

encourage His servants and to remove obstacles that human willpower alone could never budge.

Does God still work through the prayers of His people to accomplish the spread of the gospel around the world? Several years ago Sheila King Everett and her pastor-husband Randel were serving the First Baptist Church of Benton, Arkansas. A young woman in Sheila's Sunday School class who was preparing to go to Europe as a missionary with Campus Crusade for Christ requested prayer for the country of Albania. At that time Albania was totally atheistic and closed to all Christian influences. "From that time on," Sheila said, "God put it on my heart to start praying. I started praying that God would break down the walls of Albania."[6]

Not long after that, the International Mission Board of the Southern Baptist Convention began asking churches to "adopt" unreached people groups around the world. They were asked to pray that God would make a way for the gospel to be taken to a specific group or nation. One Wednesday night, Randel announced to the congregation that they had been assigned to pray for the people of Albania. "I almost shouted," Sheila said. "Some would say this was a random assignment, but I wouldn't."[7] Not long after this, the Everetts were called to serve a church in Fort Worth, Texas. There they met David and Mary Carpenter, a young professional couple, who had sold their home and left their comfortable lifestyle to prepare for what they believed was a definite call from God to share His love with the people of Albania. When they compared notes with the Everetts, the Carpenters realized that the timing of their sense of God's call was not coincidental. It coincided with Sheila's burden to pray for Albania.

In September 1992, the Carpenters finally made it to Albania. They were among the first Christian missionaries to enter that formerly-closed country. Today there are hundreds of Christian missionaries bearing witness to the gospel in that land. In the capital city of Triana, the radio tower which previously broadcast the propaganda of the Communist Party now emits a different signal as the life-giving gospel of grace sounds forth. Looking back on all this, Sheila sees a confirmation of the way prayer can make a difference in the life of an individual and in the course of a nation: "I definitely believe God uses prayer to open up the hearts of people, to open up countries that haven't been opened or ethnic groups that haven't been opened. It's made me believe in his sovereignty even that much more."[8]

PERSONAL LEARNING ACTIVITY
If God already knows everything, why then should we pray?

_____

_____

Does Grace Have Anything to Do with Worship?

During the past decade the evangelical church has been beset by a raucous controversy over the nature of public worship. Should we use praise choruses or sing only standard hymns in church? Should we use drums and guitars or only the piano and organ? Is it OK to lift your hands in worship? What about kneeling for prayer? Do we process with banners, or not process at all? Questions like these have led to "worship wars" in many places, and quite a few congregations have been torn asunder trying to deal with them. A true appreciation of the grace of God will help us to see these matters in the right perspective. Grace helps us to refocus on the main issue which is not style of music, order of worship, or some other external factor, but rather our motivation for worship and the nature of the God we dare to approach.

The prophet Malachi wrote his prophecy in response to a crisis of worship among the children of Israel. He begins by announcing a burdensome message from the Lord ("burden" is a better translation than "oracle" for the Hebrew word *na'sa* in Malachi 1:1). It is the burden of love. "'I have loved you,'

> Grace helps us to refocus on the main issue—our motivation for worship and the nature of the God we dare to approach.

God does not love us because of anything we have done for Him. He loves us freely, completely, undeservedly. This is grace!

says the Lord" (Mal. 1:2). Here we have a solemn declaration of the sovereign Lord. He has loved and chosen Israel to be His people despite their many wanderings, backslidings and sins. God's love is unconditional. He does not love them because of anything they have done for Him. He loves them freely, completely, undeservedly. This is grace!

The children of Israel made a twofold response to the love God has lavished upon them. First of all, they questioned it: "But you ask, 'How have you loved us?'" (Mal. 1:2). In other words they said to the Lord, "You don't really love us, do you God?" They questioned God's love because it is too radical and free. Their God is a contract God of wages and labor, not the covenant God of mercy and grace. Like the unhappy workers in Jesus' parable, they had made a bargain with God. They would do this if He would do that. They wanted to squeeze every possible ounce out of this deal they had made with the deity. This is the attitude they brought to worship and it led to exhaustion and compromise. When they came to God's house, they brought "defiled food" to place on His altar—crippled lambs, blind and diseased animals, the leftovers of their flock. God will not accept such offerings and He told them it would be better to close the doors of the temple completely than to carry on such a charade in His house (see v. 10). In the midst of the crisis, someone said, "Now implore God to be gracious to us" (v. 9). They had forgotten that God *was* gracious to them. They would never have returned from exile apart from God's grace. They would have no temple without God's favor and love. God did not need any of their sacrifices for He owns the cattle on a thousand hills. But the God of grace who needs nothing wants everything—their hearts, their lives, their love. This is why He would not accept their stingy sacrifices.

Once we understand who God really is, once we have experienced His inexhaustible lovingkindness, which like the dew is fresh every morning, it will change the way we worship. From a heart overflowing with gratitude, we will want to honor and glorify God by gratefully offering back to Him the many good gifts He has bestowed on us. We will not go to church to be entertained, to see "what we can get out of it" for our own private gratification, but rather to praise and worship the triune God of grace and glory.

Several years ago I taught a course on worship for students preparing to be pastors and worship leaders. I asked them to visit two congregations of contrasting worship styles and to bring back a report to the class. I shall never forget what one of the students reported. His first case study was a wealthy suburban congregation, well heeled in every way. He was welcomed avidly as a new church prospect, but he felt a kind of smugness in the worship. The church had many activities and was doing many wonderful things, but the service seemed more focused on themselves than on God. This even showed up in the morning prayer as the pastor reminded God of how busy the congregation had been in their service for Him—the building program, mission trips, the youth retreat in the Rockies, and so forth. When it was over, the student said he felt as if he had been to a pep rally or a motivational meeting.

His next assignment was a tiny African-American congregation in the inner city. The building was dilapidated and the pews uncomfortable. Here too he was warmly welcomed but he noticed a different tone in the worship. This congregation had obviously experienced a great deal of hardship and struggle, but there was a sense of joy in their singing and a note of absolute dependence on God in their prayers. This was evident in the traditional prayer-chant which began the morning service. As the whole church moaned in prayer, an elderly deacon said: "Oh Lord, I thank you that when I woke up this morning, my bed was not my cooling board, nor my blanket my winding sheet. I just want to praise you and glorify you because the blood was flowing warm through my veins. Lord, you've been so good to us. We've had enough coal to keep us warm this winter. We've had enough food to keep us from starving to death. You're an awesome God! And Lord, we're just so glad to be here this morning! We're so thankful that you let us come to this service one more time!"

Once we understand who God really is, it will change the way we worship.

Our sense of the grace of God and His omnipotent love is the foundation of biblical worship.

No one should misunderstand this real-life illustration. True worship is not a matter of rich versus poor, white versus black, or inner city versus suburban. No doubt there are inner-city churches whose worship is choked with pride and self-sufficiency, just as there are suburban churches alive with the reality of God's presence. But our sense of the grace of God, of our neediness in the face of His omnipotent love, is a true barometer of genuine spirituality and biblical worship.

PERSONAL LEARNING ACTIVITY

Think back to an especially meaningful worship service. What made it so meaningful to you?

_____

What part did grace play in that worship service?

_____

Should grace and worship be linked in our thinking and practice? Explain your answer.

_____

What Are the Marks of a Gracious Christian?

Two of the best books on living by grace are Chuck Swindoll's *Grace Awakening* and Jerry Bridge's *Transforming Grace*. Both titles point to the fact that God's grace is an active, life-changing reality. In its deepest meaning, this is what the word *gracious* connotes—not just courteous or polite, but filled with compassion, radiating kindness, winsome in all ways. This quality cannot be learned by going to a charm school nor by reading a "how-to" manual. No, it is the fruit of the Holy Spirit. It comes about when a person is grasped so thoroughly by grace that he or she becomes a channel through which God's great love shines forth in relationships with others. The more we see our own unworthiness, the more astounded we are at God's gracious favor and mercy toward us. And the more we realize that our life-purpose must be to glorify God, to please Him in every way, the more others will notice the results of God's transforming grace in our lives. They will see us shaped more and more by these five marks:

1. A Grateful Heart: The word *gratitude* comes from the Latin root *gratus,* which means "pleasing or thankful." It is closely related to the Latin word *gratia,* which means "grace." One of the surest marks of a soul touched by grace is the desire to say "thank you" to God. When Jesus healed ten men of leprosy, only one of them came back to thank Him. Jesus asked, "Where are the other nine?" (Luke 17:11-19). The other nine had been cleansed outwardly but their hearts remained tough and unchanged. We express our gratitude to God with our lives as well as our lips. The opposite of gratitude is jealousy. It stems from our thinking that somehow God has given someone else what should rightly be ours. But this is to disparage what God has given us, to consider it worthless, of no value compared to what we think we should have had. There is no place for jealousy in the family of God for we have nothing that we did not receive. Our Heavenly Father makes no mistakes in dispensing good gifts to His children.

2. A Humble Countenance: My wife and I once entertained a visiting preacher in our home. He kept saying, "I'm just a humble pastor, you know." Soon we realized that this man was bragging about his humility! But true humility is more elusive than that. Once you capture it and begin to admire it, you've already lost it. Genuine humility is a by-product of our walk with God. It is a quality others recognize in us when we ourselves may not even be aware of it. The opposite of humility is puffed-up arrogance which results from thinking more highly of ourselves than we should. As we have seen throughout this study, even the theology of grace can become an occasion for self-congratulations and pride. I have encountered this attitude on both sides of the Calvinist-

One of the surest marks of a soul touched by grace is the desire to say "thank you" to God.

Arminian divide. John Wesley and Charles Haddon Spurgeon were on opposite sides of this debate, but they both urged their followers to season their zeal for doctrinal purity with a good dose of humility. Wesley said to his disciples:

> Is it not the duty of every Arminian Preacher … never, in public or in private, to use the word *Calvinist* as a term of reproach; seeing it is neither better nor worse than calling names?—a practice no more consistent with good sense or good manners than it is with Christianity.[9]

For his part, Spurgeon recognized that many Arminians were godly Christians while some Calvinists were "as proud as Lucifer. … Far be it from me even to imagine that Zion contains none but Calvinistic Christians within her walls, or that there are none saved who do not hold our views."[10]

At the heart of our relationship with God is forgiveness.

3. A Forgiving Spirit: The glorious message of the gospel is that the Almighty God of heaven has bound Himself to lost sinners in a relationship of the freest and most perfect grace. At the heart of this relationship is forgiveness, as the psalmist knew long ago: "Blessed is he whose transgressions are forgiven, whose sins are covered. Blessed is the man whose sin the Lord does not count against him" (Ps. 32:1-2). Receiving God's forgiveness has a catalytic effect in our relationships with others. Paul makes this clear in Ephesians 4:32: "Be kind and compassionate to one another, forgiving each other, just as in Christ God forgave you." To harbor grudges against other people, to seek revenge, to bear resentment and bitterness for wrongs suffered in the past are telltale signs that one is not living by grace. The elder brother would not go into the party and rejoice at the return of his wayward sibling, and so he remained estranged from his father's love. How we relate horizontally to our brothers and sisters here on earth says a great deal about our vertical relationship with our Father in heaven (see 1 John 3:11-15).

4. A Life of Love: Over one hundred years ago Henry Drummond, the Scottish evangelist and friend of D.L. Moody, published a devotional exposition of 1 Corinthians 13. He called it *The Greatest Thing in the World*. That little book has never been out of print. It speaks powerfully of the importance of love in the Christian life. Drummond recognized that the kind of love Paul described in 1 Corinthians 13 is not a mere human achievement but rather a graciously given divine gift. It is not something we have the capacity to produce on our own, but only the capacity to receive it by God's grace. Even so, Drummond said, Christian love is an effect, the cause of which is God's extraordinary love for us.

Contemplate the love of Christ–and you will love.

"We love—because He first loved us." Look at that word "because." It is the cause of which I have spoken. "Because He first loved us," the effect follows that we love, we love him, we love all men. We cannot help it. Because he loved us, we love, we love everybody. Our heart is slowly changed. Contemplate the love of Christ, and you will love. Stand before that mirror, reflect Christ's character, and you will be changed into the same image from tenderness to tenderness. There is no other way. You cannot love to order. You can only look at the lovely object, and fall in love with it, and grow into likeness to it.[11]

A life of love will reflect a proper balance between grace and truth. Some Christians are big on grace but soft on truth. They glide over the Bible's warnings about the wrath of God and the future judgment that awaits those who reject Christ. On the other hand, there are some other Christians who are great champions of truth, but they have little to say about grace. They are straight laced in doctrine, but they wear their convictions like a straight jacket! They have not learned how to relax into grace. Nor have they learned the wisdom of the late Francis Schaeffer who reminded us that "we must not forget that the final end is not what we are against, but what we are for."[12] A gracious life marked by love has ample room for both grace and truth. Neither need be sacrificed for the other for they are not enemies but friends.

5. A Passion for Souls: Throughout this study we have emphasized the congruence and compatibility of God's sovereignty in salvation on the one hand and the responsibility, indeed the duty, of human beings to repent and believe the gospel on the other. No one has said this better than J.C. Ryle, a great Christian leader in 19th-century England:

> Everywhere in Scripture it is a leading principle that man can lose his own soul, that if he is lost at last it will be his own fault, and his blood will be on his own head. The same inspired Bible which reveals this doctrine of Election is the Bible which contains the words, "Why will ye die, O house of Israel?"—"Ye will not come unto me, that ye might have life."—"This is the condemnation, that light has come into the world, and men loved darkness rather than light, because their deeds were evil" (Ezekiel 18:31; John 5:40; 3:19). The Bible never says that sinners miss heaven because they are not Elect, but because they "neglect the great salvation," and because they will not repent and believe.[13]

Every believer is called to be a witness of His grace.

Knowing this to be true, every Christian whose life has been changed by the grace of God is called to be a witness of Jesus Christ to the lost. Of course, we cannot save or convert anyone; that is God's business. Nor are we responsible for making up the content of the message out of our own heads. God has clearly revealed the good news of salvation in His infallible Word. The Bible is God's love letter to a lost world. We are in the delivery business. Our job is to make sure that God's love letter is delivered to its intended recipients—and that means every single person in the world. But unlike a regular mail carrier who has (or should have) no particular interest in the mail he carries, we have a vital interest both in the message we deliver and in the response of those to whom we present it. It was said of the great Puritan pastor Richard Baxter that he preached as a dying man to dying men. A passion for souls is one of the indelible marks of a gracious Christian.

PERSONAL LEARNING ACTIVITY

The author suggests that there are five marks of a life being transformed by God's grace. They are:

___ 1. A grateful heart

___ 2. A humble countenance

___ 3. A forgiving spirit

___ 4. A life of love

___ 5. A passion for souls

Place a check mark by the ones where you are strong. Place an asterisk by the ones where you need improvement. What must happen for you to experience growth in all these areas?

_____

_____

Living the Benediction

It is appropriate that we close this study of the doctrine of grace with a benediction, a word of blessing. And there is none better than what Paul wrote at the conclusion of his second Letter to the Corinthian Christians: "May the grace of the Lord Jesus Christ, and the love of God, and the fellowship of the Holy Spirit be with you all" (13:14). This verse sums up the great drama of redemption from first to last. We focus first on the grace of our Lord Jesus Christ, the divine Son of God who left the security of the Father's bosom in heaven to be born of a virgin here on earth. In His life and through His death on the cross, He perfectly fulfilled all the righteous demands of God's law-making atonement through the shedding of His blood. At His resurrection on Easter Sunday He burst asunder the bonds of death. He ascended back to heaven where He waits at the Father's side ready to come again in final triumph when the time is right. And what is the source of these mighty acts of grace? Nothing less than the free and

Our salvation in Christ is based on nothing less than the free and radical love of God the Father.

radical love of God the Father. And how do we participate in such love? Through the ministry of the Holy Spirit who convicts and regenerates us, seals and indwells us, fills and empowers us for the journey of faith to which we are called.

When the angels in heaven consider all that this means, they must gasp with wonder. When we who are not merely onlookers but beneficiaries of such amazing grace attempt to contemplate its full meaning, surely we too are filled with overwhelming wonder, gratitude, and praise—breathlessly so. Charles Wesley said it best in the last verse of his great hymn, "And Can It Be":

'Tis mystery all! The Immortal dies!
Who can explore His strange design?
In vain the first-born seraph tries
To sound the depths of love divine!
'Tis mercy all! let earth adore,
Let angel minds inquire no more.[14]

Sola Gratia!

Soli Deo Gloria!

[1]C.H. Spurgeon, *The Metropolitan Tabernacle Pulpit* (Pasadena, TX: Pilgrim Publications, 1977), vol. XLVIII, 274.
[2]George Whitefield, *Journals* (London: The Banner of Truth Trust, 1960), 47.
[3]Augustus M. Toplady, "Rock of Ages."
[4]As quoted in Lewis B. Smedes, *Shame and Grace* (New York: HarperCollins Publishers, 1993), 111.
[5]T.W. Hunt, *The Doctrine of Prayer* (Nashville, TN: Convention Press, 1986), 8.
[6]n.a., "Albania's access to gospel attributed to prayer," *Alabama Baptist,* 14 Oct. 1999: 4.
[7]Ibid.
[8]Ibid.
[9]John Wesley, *The Works of John Wesley* (Peabody, Mass: Hendrickson Publishers, Inc., n.d.), third edition, 360-361.
[10]Iain H. Murray, *The Forgotten Spurgeon* (Carlisle, PA: The Banner of Truth Trust, 1966), 65.
[11]Henry Drummond, *The Greatest Thing in the World* (Birmingham, AL: Samford University Press, 1997), 57-58.
[12]As quoted in Ibid., xiii.
[13]John Charles Ryle, *Old Paths* (Cambridge, James Clarke & Co., Ltd., 1972), 468.
[14]Charles Wesley, "The Christian Life."

CHRISTIAN GROWTH STUDY PLAN

Preparing Christians to Serve

In the **Christian Growth Study Plan (formerly Church Study Course),** this book *Amazing Grace* is a resource for course credit in the subject area Baptist Doctrine of the Christian Growth category of diploma plans. To receive credit, read the book, complete the learning activities, show your work to your pastor, a staff member or church leader, then complete the following information. This page may be duplicated. Send the completed page to:

Christian Growth Study Plan
127 Ninth Avenue, North, MSN 117
Nashville, TN 37234-0117
FAX: (615)251-5067

For information about the Christian Growth Study Plan, refer to the current Christian Growth Study Plan Catalog. Your church office may have a copy. If not, request a free copy from the Christian Growth Study Plan office (615/251-2525).

Amazing Grace
COURSE NUMBER: CG-0600

PARTICIPANT INFORMATION

Social Security Number (USA ONLY)	Personal CGSP Number*	Date of Birth (MONTH, DAY, YEAR)
- -	-	- -

Name (First, Middle, Last)	Home Phone
	- -

Address (Street, Route, or P.O. Box)	City, State, or Province	Zip/Postal Code

CHURCH INFORMATION

Church Name

Address (Street, Route, or P.O. Box)	City, State, or Province	Zip/Postal Code

CHANGE REQUEST ONLY

☐ Former Name		
☐ Former Address	City, State, or Province	Zip/Postal Code
☐ Former Church	City, State, or Province	Zip/Postal Code

Signature of Pastor, Conference Leader, or Other Church Leader	Date

*New participants are requested but not required to give SS# and date of birth. Existing participants, please give CGSP# when using SS# for the first time. Thereafter, only one ID# is required. **Mail to:** Christian Growth Study Plan, 127 Ninth Ave., North, Nashville, TN 37234-0117. Fax: (615)251-5067

Rev. 6-99